FIRST WE READ, THEN WE WRITE

First We Read, Then We Write

EMERSON ON THE CREATIVE PROCESS

By Robert D. Richardson

UNIVERSITY OF IOWA PRESS
Iowa City

UNIVERSITY OF IOWA PRESS, IOWA CITY 52242
www.uiowapress.org
Printed in the United States of America

Design by Teresa W. Wingfield

The University of Iowa Press is a member of Green Press Initiative and is committed to preserving natural resources.

Printed on acid-free paper

LIBRARY OF CONGRESS CATALOGING-IN-PUBLICATION DATA

Richardson, Robert D., 1934–
    First we read, then we write: Emerson on the creative process / by Robert D. Richardson
        p.   cm.
    Includes bibliographical references and index.
    ISBN: 978-1-58729-793-9 (cloth)
    ISBN: 978-1-60938-347-3 (pbk)
    1. Emerson, Ralph Waldo, 1803–1882.   2. Emerson, Ralph Waldo, 1803–1882—Knowledge and learning.   3. Authors, American—19th century—Biography.   4. Books and reading.   5. Creative writing.   6. Creation (Literary, artistic, etc.)   I. Title.
    PS1631.R54 2009
    814'.3—dc22   2008040554

For Lissa, for Anne, and for Cody Rose

What seas what shores what grey rocks and what islands
What water lapping the bow
And scent of pine and the woodthrush singing
    through the fog
What images return
O my daughter[s].

—T. S. ELIOT, "MARINA"

Contents

Foreword

JOHN BANVILLE

Robert Richardson is that rarest of phenomena, a historian and biographer gifted with the ability to communicate enthusiasm. To read him is to appreciate the full import of that word: we feel *enthousiasmos*, inspired, breathed into, by the transcendent power of ideas and language. His great trio of biographies, of Emerson, Thoreau and William James, constitutes one of the landmarks of American literature in the twentieth century. *Emerson: The Mind on Fire* is perhaps his finest achievement so far, and *First We Read, Then We Write* might be considered the distillation of his thinking on Emerson as literary exemplar.

In this deceptively modest volume Richardson is intent on setting his subject before us not so much as a philosopher—Emerson's philosophical achievement is taken as recognized—but as a model writer to be profitably emulated by all who would follow the same trade, especially the beginner. His second major theme is that of Emerson the creative reader. In that marvellous essay "The American Scholar," Emerson insists that there is creative reading as well as creative writing, and adds, beautifully, "When the mind is braced by labor and invention, the page of whatever book we read becomes luminous with manifold allusion."

Along with his learning, which is prodigious, Richardson writes a wonderfully fluent, agile prose; he has a poet's sense of nuance and a novelist's grasp of dramatic rhythm; he also has a positive genius for apposite quotation, as we see over and again in *First We Read*. Can there be any more *exciting* critical writing than this?

Richardson is as accommodating as Emerson himself, and sets out by quoting that splendid piece of encouragement, again from "The American Scholar," in which Emerson speaks of "meek young men" who sit in libraries reading books by Cicero, Locke, and Bacon in the gloomy conviction that they must accept unquestioningly the views of these great men, "forgetful that Cicero, Locke, and Bacon were only young men in libraries when they wrote those books."

One of the main sources of excitement when we read Emerson is the spectacle of a man being repeatedly swept away by his own conception of himself and his capacities. Richardson in his introduction to the present volume notes how we find Emerson as a young man writing in his journal and picking out the proverbs of Solomon and the essays of Bacon and Montaigne and declaring, with the oblivious arrogance of youth: "I should like to add another volume to this valuable work."

Emerson has suffered the fate of all eminently quotable writers, in that much of what he wrote has suffered the distortion of seeming to have been written not by a human hand holding a pen in his fingers but by a stonemason hammering a chisel. As Richardson points out, however, Emerson in his day was first and foremost a lecturer: "His essays all began as lectures. His writing was first speaking." This point cannot be made strongly enough or too often. Within every line that Emerson wrote, the rhythm of the spoken word beats like a heart.

Although Emerson was only seven when his father died, there was one happy result of the tragedy, in that the boy was brought up by his sensible and intelligent mother, with the active, on occasion perhaps too active, assistance of his redoubtable Aunt Mary Moody Emerson. This vigorous and intellectually restless spinster lived for periods in the Emerson family home and wielded a deep influence on the young Waldo—the two carried on a sprightly and frequently profound correspondence until Aunt Mary's death in 1863. It is surely not fanciful to see in Emerson's unique combination of practicality and speculative adventurousness the marks of his upbringing under the not at all constricting wings of these two capable and independent-minded women.

Richardson points out that for Emerson "the sentence—not the paragraph and not the essay—is the main structural and formal unit." This is the most striking characteristic of Emerson's remarkable prose, and accounts for the fireworks quality of his style as well as its peculiar difficulties. "Pushed as far as he pushed them," Richardson remarks, "many of Emerson's sentences stand out by themselves, alone and exposed like scarecrows in a cornfield . . . ."

For Emerson there is no such thing as escapist reading. His own way with books was gloriously slapdash. He read anything and everything, without system—but then, in his philosophy he was as great an anti-systematiser as Nietzsche—and flicked cavalierly through the most urgently demanding tomes, picking up in magpie-fashion the more glittering ideas and observations. Speaking to a younger admirer, he cautioned that "reading long at one time anything, no matter how it fascinates, destroys thought as completely as the inflections forced by external causes." He also advised him to "Stop if you find yourself becoming absorbed, at even the first paragraph," and urged that he should "learn to divine books, to *feel* those that you want without wasting much time over them. . . . The glance reveals what the gaze obscures."

And when the reading is done, there is the writing. Emerson, with that sense of desperation and near-panic that Richardson identifies as one of the main spurs of his work, always saw writing as an act that is as much physical as mental, a venture into the real world and not a mere spinning of castles in the vacant air of the mind. Richardson singles out as the best piece of practical advice Emerson ever gave to anyone wishing to write this typically violent and risk-laden directive: "The way to write is to throw your body at the mark when your arrows are spent."

Emerson, as Richardson reminds us, took the writer to be among "the great class, they who affect our imagination, the men who could not make their hands meet around their objects, the rapt, the lost, the fools of ideas." And of course, he was himself one of the leaders. Richardson observes that "in every admonition [about writing] we hear his willingness to confront his own failures; indeed, he never seems more than a few inches from utter calamity."

This is why Emerson's work thrills us, challenges us, even frightens us, a little. For him, all is doing, all is risk. In his essay, "Experience," he famously writes: "Life only avails, not the having lived. Power ceases in the instant of repose; it resides in the moment of transition from a past to a new state, in the shooting of the gulf, in the darting to an aim." The writer, as we recognize, does it all twice, first lives—and reads!—then writes. Emerson knows well but does not reck the cost: "A writer must live and die by his writing. Good for that and good for nothing else." Has there ever been a more bracingly harsh prescription to the writer, or a more uncompromising statement of the writer's vocation?

In this brief, elegant, and quietly passionate volume Robert Richardson has produced an invaluable handbook both for the experienced writer and aspirant. A copy of it should be presented to every student at the commencement of every writing class in every college around the world. For it is a serious course the beginner is embarked on, in which he or she must learn to write not in the hope of expressing a puny self but to be, among other things, a guardian of language. The poet, Emerson himself tells us, "Is representative. He stands among partial men for the complete man, and apprises us not of his wealth, but of the commonwealth." As Robert Richardson reiterates on every page of this book, to be a writer is a noble calling, which calls for noble sacrifice, even in the prosaic times in which we live, read and write.

FIRST WE READ, THEN WE WRITE

Introduction

The first sentence of Ralph Waldo Emerson's that reached me still jolts me every time I run into it. "Meek young men," he wrote in "The American Scholar," "grow up in libraries believing it their duty to accept the views which Cicero, which Locke, which Bacon have given, forgetful that Cicero, Locke, and Bacon were only young men in libraries when they wrote those books."

Writing was the central passion of Emerson's life. He considered himself a poet; he wrote what is arguably the best piece ever written on expressionism in literature—an essay called "The Poet"; he wrote about writers—Goethe, Shakespeare, Montaigne and he talked and wrote, especially in his journals, about the art and the craft of writing. But he never wrote an essay on writing.

One reason he never did may have been that he had impossible, unreachable ambitions as a writer himself. At age twenty-one he turned uncertainly to graduate study in divinity. He found himself longing for the open horizons and welcoming fields of endeavor enjoyed by earlier generations, and longing for a time when entering contestants "were never troubled with libraries of names and dates." Like many a beginning grad student, he felt "life is wasted in the necessary preparation of finding what is the true way, and we die just as we enter it." Graduate study in divinity in 1824, even for a Unitarian, meant almost entirely Bible study; by July, Emerson was reading Nathaniel Lardner's *History of the Apostles and Evangelists* and studying the book of Proverbs in the Old Testament. Proverbs is not a gospel, and it is not a great narrative like Genesis. It is a very minor book, though it does have a prophetic voice and it sits near Ecclesiastes, the Song of Solomon, and Isaiah in the canon. Emerson's heart rose at the prospect of the passive study of scripture. It was his ambition not to annotate but to *write* one of "those books which collect and embody the wisdom of their times." Emerson looked on Solomon as a fellow writer, someone to be imitated, not just venerated. The young Emerson singled out in his journal the proverbs of Solomon, and Bacon's and Montaigne's essays, and declared, "I should like to add another volume to this valuable work." Preposterous as this must appear to the orthodox Christian, it made plain sense to Emerson. But, we say incredulously, what if it was God who was speaking through Solomon? Well, perhaps he would speak through Emerson also.

It was an aspiration he would claim at age twenty-one only in his private journal, but which he would reclaim, albeit collectively, in the last paragraph of the final essay in his 1850 book *Representative Men* almost thirty years later. "We too must write Bibles," he writes at the end of his essay on Goethe. His ambition then, from the start, was as phenomenal as it was unwavering.

We may debate his success, but as his young friend Henry Thoreau noted, "in the long run men hit only what they aim at." Emerson also knew, as Epictetus knew, that "all things have two handles. Beware of the wrong one." And the Proverbs of Solomon are themselves darkly eloquent about taking the wrong path:

I went by the field of the slothful, and by the vineyard of the
    man void of understanding:
And, lo, it was all grown over with thorns, and nettles had
    covered the face thereof, and the stone wall thereof was
    broken down.
Then I saw, and considered it well: I looked upon it, and
    received instruction.
Yet a little sleep, a little slumber, a little folding of the hands
    to sleep:
So shall thy poverty come as one that travelleth, and thy
    want as an armed man. (PROVERBS 24:30–34)

Emerson's immodest—almost indecent—ambition seems both too high and too abstract to be real, or to be believed; but there was always another side to the man, a side where both his feet are planted in everyday reality, a side of him that often sounds overwhelmed, sometimes desperate, but always determined. A person, he wrote, "must do the work with that faculty he has now. But that faculty is the accumulation of past days. No rival can rival backwards. What you have learned and done is safe and fruitful. Work and learn in evil days, in insulted days, in days of debt and depression and calamity. Fight best in the shade of the cloud of arrows."

It is encouraging to learn that writing was often a desperate struggle for Emerson. He came early to the knowledge that every day is the Day of Creation as well as the Day of Judgment. At day's end he never felt he had done his best, never felt he had achieved adequate expression. His best poem, "Days," expresses his sense of the accusing sufficiency of every single day and his chagrined feeling that he was not making the best use of his time, that he was claiming the wrong gifts, working the wrong side of the street, and that every day shut down for him on a night of failure.

> Daughters of Time, the hypocritic Days,
> Muffled and dumb like barefoot dervishes,
> And marching single in an endless file,
> Bring diadems and fagots in their hands.
> To each they offer gifts after his will,
> Bread, kingdoms, stars, and sky that holds them all.
> I, in my pleached garden, watched the pomp,
> Forgot my morning wishes, hastily
> Took a few herbs and apples, and the Day
> Turned and departed silent. I, too late,
> Under her solemn fillet saw the scorn.

Out of his own repeated failures—from which, however, he arose each morning ready to try again—Emerson carved sentences of useful, practical advice, mostly for himself, one gathers, but fit for anyone to put up over a writing desk or write on the flyleaf of a new notebook. Emerson's preferred unit of composition is the sentence, not the paragraph and certainly not the essay. He wrote some of the best sentences in English; a surprising number are about writing good sentences.

> The first rule of writing is not to omit the thing you meant to say.
> Good writing and brilliant conversation are perpetual allegories.

All writing should be selection in order to drop every dead
     word.
The thing set down in words is not therefore affirmed. It
     must affirm itself or no forms of grammar and no verisi-
     militude can give evidence; and no array of arguments.
Contagion, yeast, "emptins" [yeasty lees of beer or cider],
     anything to convey fermentation, import fermentation,
     induce fermentation into a quiescent mass, inspiration,
     by virtue or vice, by friend or fiend, angels or "gin."
All that can be thought can be written.

Perhaps this last was true in a general way, but how well
could the actual Emerson write what he thought? Always
he held up his doings—his writing and his life—to the great
standard, that is, to nature. "When I look at the sweeping
sleet amid the pinewoods, my sentences look very contemptible." But if his writing always had one foot planted in nature,
the other foot rested, if somewhat lightly, on his wide and
eager reading.

Reading

"There is then creative reading as well as creative writing," Emerson says in "The American Scholar." "First we eat, then we beget; first we read, then we write." Reading is creative for Emerson; it is also active. In "History" he insists that "the student is to read history actively and not passively; to esteem his own life the text, and books the commentary." All Emerson's comments about reading aim to strengthen the authority of readers (and writers) of books, and to weaken or lighten the authority of books themselves. In an unpublished late essay called "Subjectiveness," he put it with compressed simplicity. While you are reading, he said, "you are the book's book."

His best comments on reading are about its limits and dangers. He was as suspicious of reading as he was of traveling. Escapist reading was, he thought, a fool's paradise. He liked Hobbes for saying, "if I had read as much as other men I should be as ignorant." He especially admired Montaigne, who had learned not to overvalue books. "If I am a man of some reading, I am a man of no retention," Montaigne wrote cheerfully. "I do not bite my nails about the difficulties I meet with in my reading. . . . I do nothing without gaiety. . . . My sight is confounded and dissipated by poring."

Emerson's critique of reading makes sense, however, only if we understand that he himself was a prodigious and inveterate reader, a man in love with and addicted to books. He seems to have read everything. He habitually read all the British magazines, all the American ones, and all the new books as they came out. Besides the predictable reading in the Greek and Roman classics, in the history and literature of England, France, and Germany, and in the Judeo-Christian tradition, he read the literature and scriptures of India, China, and Persia. He studied Buddhism, Hinduism, Confucianism, Zoroastrianism, and Islam. He read books on Russia, on the South Seas, on agriculture and fruit trees, on painting and music. He read novels, poems, plays, and biographies. He read newspapers, travel books, and government reports.

He generally took more books out of the library than he was able to read before they were due back. His charging records at the Boston Athenaeum, the Harvard College Library, and the Boston Society Library are not so much a measure of his intake as of his appetite. He glanced at thousands of books. He read carefully many hundreds that caught his attention. He returned over and over to a favorite few, including Montaigne, Plutarch, Plato, Plotinus, Goethe, de Stael, and Wordsworth.

Emerson once noted that Coleridge had identified four classes of readers: the hourglass, the sponge, the jelly-bag, and the Golconda. The hourglass gives back everything it takes in, unchanged. The sponge gives back everything it takes in, only a little dirtier. The jelly-bag squeezes out the valuable and keeps the worthless, while the Golconda runs everything through a sieve, keeping only the nuggets. Emerson was the Golconda reader par excellence, or what American miners call a "high-grader"—a person who goes through a mine and pockets only the richest lumps of ore.

Reading was a physical necessity for Emerson. "I do not feel as if my day had substance in it, if I have read nothing," he once wrote a friend. "I expect a man to be a great reader," he wrote on another occasion, "or in proportion to the spontaneous power, should be the assimilating power." He knew at first hand the power a book can have. "Many times the reading of a book has made the fortune of the reader,—has decided his way of life. The reading of voyages and travels has waked a boy's ambition and curiosity and made him a sailor and an explorer of new countries all his life, a powerful merchant, a good soldier, a pure patriot, or a successful student of science." Of the books which had moved him personally he could write with open gratitude and a clear sense of feeling transported. Of Montaigne's *Essays* he said: "It seemed to me as if I had written the book myself in some former life. . . . No book before or since was ever so much to me as that." When he sent his friend Sam Ward a copy of Augustine's *Confessions*, he wrote:

> I push the little antiquity toward you merely out of gratitude to some golden words I read in it last summer. What better oblation could I offer to the Saint than the opportunity of a new proselyte? But do not read. Why read this or any book? It is a foolish conformity and does well for dead people. It happens to us once or twice in a lifetime to be drunk with some book which probably has some extraordinary relative power to intoxicate *us* and none other; and having exhausted that cup of enchantment we go groping in libraries all our years afterwards in the hope of being in Paradise again.

Considering that Emerson was a confirmed and habitual reader, he sometimes seems to protest too much. "It is taking a great liberty with a man to offer to lend him a book," he once noted. "Each of the books I read invades me, displaces me." Often there is a comic note to his self-admonitions. After reading a book about German literature by Wolfgang Menzel, he wrote: "I surprised you, O Waldo Emerson, yesterday eve, hurrying up one page and down another of a little book of some Menzel, panting and straining after the sense of some mob better or worse of German authors. I thought you had known better. Adhere, sit fast, lie low." But only those who are swamped in books—and thus dealing continually with the views of others—have to worry much about guarding their personal integrity. It is precisely the reader of many books who is in danger of losing sight of his own views, and of becoming, as Emerson says, "drugged with books for want of wisdom."

Emerson liked to give the impression that he was an uncommitted and indiscriminate reader. "If a man reads a book because it interests him and reads in all directions for the same reason, his reading is pure and interests me," he once said. "No matter where you begin, read anything for five hours a day and you will soon be knowing." Yet however much he read, there were whole categories of books the mature Emerson would not read. He would not read theology or academic controversy. He wanted original accounts, first-hand experience, personal witness. He would read your poem or your novel, but not your opinion of someone else's poem or novel, let alone your opinion of someone else's opinion. An early lecture records his characteristic and disquieting bluntness on this subject: "A vast number of books are written in quiet imitation of the old civil, ecclesiastical and literary history; of these we need take no account. They are written by the dead to be read by the dead."

Many books acquired only a temporary hold on him. "How many centers have we fondly found, which proved soon to be circumferential points! How many conversations on books seemed epochs, at the moment, which we have now actually forgotten." He never used his reading as an anodyne. He fretted if he wasn't getting something all the time. "We are too civil to books," he complained. "For a few golden sentences we will turn over and actually read a volume of 4 or 5 hundred pages."

The most persistent problem Emerson had with books was that they exerted too great, not too little, an influence on him. Books were a major part of the baggage he carried in what he once called "the knapsack of custom." "The public necessarily picks out for the emulation of the young the Oberlins, the Wesleys, Dr. Lowell and Dr. Ware. But with worst effect. All this excellence beforehand kills their own. They ought to come out to their work ignorant that ever another had wrought. Imitation cannot go above its model."

As much as Emerson recognized the claims of the classics ("It is always an economy of time to read old books"), he opposed the passive ingestion and approval of canonical texts just because they were famous. "If Homer is that man he is taken for, he has not yet done his office when he has educated the learned of Europe for a thousand years. He is now to approve himself a master of delight to me also. If he cannot do that, all his fame shall avail him nothing."

Emerson did not read in order to pick up the common coin of his culture or class. He did not even read with the Arnoldian hope of learning the best that had been thought and said. Emerson read for personal gain, for personal use.

"A man must teach himself," he observed, "because he can only read according to his state." Like Stephen Dedalus, Emerson retained "nothing of all he read save that which seemed to him an echo or a prophecy of his own state." He put it in other ways: "For only that book can we read which relates to me something that is already in my mind." He had a full awareness of this in his earliest lectures. "What can we see, read, acquire but what we are?" he asked in "Ethics" in 1835. "You have seen a skilful man reading Plutarch. Well, that author is a thousand things to a thousand persons. Take that book into your own two hands and read your eyes out. You will never find there what the other finds. . . . Or do you think you can possibly hear and bring away from any conversation more than is already in your mind born or ready to be born?" Emerson read explicitly the way we all read implicitly. "Insist that the Schelling, Schleiermacher, Ackerman or whoever propounds to you a mythology, is only a more or less awkward translation of entities in your own consciousness. . . . If Spinoza cannot [render back to you your own consciousness], perhaps Kant will." This is not, of course, to deny new thoughts or the original contributions of others. It is just an assertion that we can follow an argument and recognize its strength only by its congruence with our own mental processes.

When we read actively, we can profit from anything. "A good head cannot read amiss," said Emerson. "In every book he finds passages which seem confidences or asides, hidden from all else, and unmistakeably meant for his ear. No book has worth by itself, but by the relation to what you have from many other books, it weighs." It was in this frame of mind that Emerson could claim: "It makes no difference what I read. If it is irrelevant I read it deeper. I read it until it is pertinent to me and mine, to nature and to the hour that now passes. A good scholar will find Aristophanes and Hafiz and Rabelais full of American History."

What Emerson claimed for himself, he was ready to extend to others. He was reluctant to speak of *the* meaning of a book, and eager to affirm the idea that there would be as many meanings of a book as it had readers. "Every word we speak is million-faced or convertible to an indefinite number of applications. If it were not so, we could read no book. Your remark would fit only your own case not mine. And Dante who described his circumstance would be unintelligible now. But a thousand readers in a thousand different years shall read his story and find it a picture of their story by making of course a new application of every word." It is precisely this convertibility of words that, far from separating us, makes reading and writing possible in the first place.

Emerson himself read almost entirely in order to feed his writing. "Everything a man knows and does enters into and modifies his expression of himself," he wrote in an early journal. A few years later he commented: "Philosophers must not write history for me. They know too much. I read some Plutarch or even dull Belknap or Williamson and in their dry dead annals I get thoughts which they never put there. . . . Do not they say that the highest joy is the creator's not the receiver's?" He responded enthusiastically to Goethe's frank recognition of the importance of assimilation to the writer. "What is genius," Goethe had said, "but the faculty of seizing and turning to account everything that strikes us?" Goethe insisted that "the greatest genius will never be worth much if he pretends to draw exclusively from his own resources," and that "every one of my writings has been furnished to me by a thousand different persons, a thousand different things."

Reading and writing were favorite topics for Emerson. In essays, letters, and journals he returns again and again to both subjects. He liked to talk about them, too, as we can see in a series of remarkably unguarded conversations he had between 1865 and 1870 with a young Williams College student named Charles Woodbury. Woodbury listened carefully, took notes, and wrote down much of what Emerson talked about, eventually publishing it as *Talks with Ralph Waldo Emerson* in 1890. Woodbury went on from Williams to become a successful oil merchant in San Francisco. He lived in Oakland and was active in Unitarian circles, even writing the occasional original hymn. That Woodbury was not a writer gives his account a special interest; he seems to have made little effort to clean up Emerson's talk, in which ideas and images just tumble out, and we hear the man himself, sitting in Woodbury's college room, talking books.

"Reading is closely related to writing. While the mind is plastic there should be care as to its impressions. The new facts should come from nature, fresh, buoyant, inspiring, exact. Later in life, when there is less danger of imitating those traits of expression through which information has been received, facts may be gleaned from a wider field. But now you shall not read these books"—pointing— "Prescott or Bancroft or Motley. Prescott is a thorough man. Bancroft reads enormously, always understands his subject. Motley is painstaking, but too mechanical. So are they all. Their style slays. Neither of them lifts himself off his feet. They have no lilt in them. You noticed the marble we have just seen? You remember that marble is nothing but crystallized limestone? Well, some writers never get out of that limestone condition."

Emerson told Woodbury to read writers "who are not lazy; who put themselves into contact with the realities. So you learn to look with your eyes too. And do not forget the Persian, Parsee, and Hindoo religious books—the Avesta, Vendidad, and the rest; books of travel too." Emerson gave Woodbury lots of names of authors and titles. He recommended Bacon and Berkeley, Sharon Turner and Plutarch. "And there is Darwin! I am glad to see him here." But where Emerson really came alive was when he talked bluntly and forcefully about what *not* to read. "Avoid all second-hand borrowing books—'Collections of——,' 'Beauties of——,' etc. I see you have some on your shelves. I would burn them. No one can select the beautiful passages of another for you. It is beautiful for him—well! Another thought, wedding your aspirations, will be the thing of beauty for you. Do your own quarrying."

"Did you ever think about the logic of stimulus?" Emerson asked Woodbury. "There is a great secret in knowing what to keep out of the mind as well as what to put in." Emerson used newspapers as an example. He thought no one should neglect them. "But have little to do with them. Learn to get *their* best too, without their getting yours. Do not read when the mind is creative. And do not read thoroughly, column by column. Remember they are made for everybody, and don't try to get what isn't meant for you." Emerson's advice to Woodbury is not empty exhortation. He is describing his own reading habits. "Reading long at one time anything, no matter how it fascinates, destroys thought as completely as the inflections forced by external causes. Do not permit this. Stop if you find yourself becoming absorbed, at even the first paragraph."

The logic behind Emerson's apparent disparaging of reading is the logic of a person who expects his reading to be useful above all. "Do not attempt to be a great reader," Emerson tells Woodbury. "And read for facts and not by the bookful. You must know about ownership in facts. What another sees and tells you is not yours, but his." The reader is to take only what really suits him. Emerson tells Woodbury he ought to "learn to divine books, to *feel* those that you want without wasting much time over them. Remember you must know only the excellent of all that has been presented. But often a chapter is enough. The glance reveals what the gaze obscures." When pressed for details on exactly how to do this, Emerson hesitated a moment, Woodbury says, and then went on: "Well, learn how to tell from the beginning of the chapters and from glimpses of the sentences whether you need to read them entirely through. So turn page after page, keeping your writer's thought before you, but not tarrying with him, until he has brought you the thing you are in search of; then dwell with him, if so be he has what you want. But recollect you only read to start your own team."

Most writers eventually disappear into their texts; many aim to do so. Emerson aimed at the opposite. His faith in texts is a faith only in their carrying capacity. His theory of reading and his theory of writing are both biographical; the text should carry the reader to the writer, and should carry the writer to the reader. Conventional argumentation frowns on ad hominem arguments. For Emerson it is just the other way. All arguments are ad hominem or ad feminam; nothing else matters. When the connection is made between writer and reader, the text dissolves into the connection. The best texts do this over and over.

The awestruck but perceptive young Woodbury observed that it was symbolic that Henry Ward Beecher, the famous orator and preacher, had a huge wheel-shaped desk, at the center of which sat Beecher himself. Emerson, by contrast, worked in a rocking chair that he pulled up to the edge of a round writing table. What Emerson knew was that while things are circular ("unit and universe are round") and while every person is his or her own center, no one is the center of the whole world. "Every spirit builds itself a house, and beyond its house a world, and beyond its world a heaven," he says at the end of *Nature*. "Know then, that the world exists for you. For you is the phenomenon perfect. What we are, that only can we see." Then he goes on to say, "Build, therefore, your own world." He might just as well have said: "Read and write, therefore, your own world," since creative reading was at last inseparable for him from creative writing. But reading was just the means. The end—the purpose—was writing.

Keeping a Journal

The mature Emerson would look back on his voluminous journals as his savings bank. The phrase from the world of money seems feeble; it lacks the disastrous felicity—as Kenneth Burke called it—of, say, William James's insistence on the "cash value of an idea," but Emerson's journals served a more vital purpose when he was just starting out. "Keep a journal . . . for the habit of rendering account to yourself of yourself in some rigorous manner and at more certain intervals than mere conversation." What Emerson kept, and what he recommended enthusiastically to others, were what used to be called commonplace books, blank bound volumes in which one writes down vivid images, great descriptions, striking turns of phrase, ideas, high points from one's life and reading—things one wants to remember and hold on to. A commonplace book is not a diary, an appointment calendar, or a record of one's feelings. If your journal consists of the best moments of your life and reading, then rereading it will be like walking a high mountain trail that goes from peak to peak without the intervening descent into the trough of routine. Just reading in such a journal of high points will tighten your strings and raise your pitch.

Emerson pushed journal-keeping on his closest friends. The opening entry of Henry Thoreau's journal, dated October 22, 1837, records laconically a meeting between the twenty-year-old Thoreau and the thirty-four-year-old Emerson. "'What are you doing now?' he asked. 'Do you keep a journal?' So I make my first entry today."

Emerson cared enough about journal-keeping to describe his initial effort and why it failed:

> When I was quite young I fancied that by keeping a Manuscript Journal by me, over whose pages I wrote a list of the great topics of human study, as, Religion, Poetry, Politics, Love, etc, in the course of a few years I should be able to complete a sort of Encyclopedia containing the net value of all the definitions at which the world had arrived. But at the end of a couple of years my Cabinet Cyclopedia though much enlarged was no nearer completeness than on its first day. Nay, somehow the whole plan of it needed alteration.

It is always helpful to hear from another what doesn't work. Then, when that person talks about what does work, he or she has some credit in our eyes. Emerson abandoned the system of predetermined subject headings. He explained his new system to Elizabeth Peabody, who passed it on in a letter to her brother, George: "He advised me to keep a manuscript book and write down every train of thought which arose on any interesting subject with the imagery in which it first came into my mind. This manuscript was to be perfectly informal and allow of skipping from one subject to another with only a black line between. After it was written I could run a heading of subjects over the top—and when I wanted to make up an article—*there* were all my thoughts, *ready*." Emerson should have added—or perhaps Peabody forgot—that you have to index each journal in the back so you can find all the entries on a given subject without having to read through the entire journal each time you want to find something. Just as Sharon Cameron has argued that Thoreau's journal is his greatest achievement, so it can be argued that Emerson's journals are his greatest, preserving as they do the play of mind, the ever-changing focus, the wide sympathies, the unconventionality of Emerson's mind in its first encounters with events, books, and people. And always he expected more of it than it could possibly deliver. With comical self-deprecation he told his friend Thomas Carlyle, "My Journals, which I dot at here at home day by day, are full of disjointed dreams, audacities, unsystematic irresponsible lampoons of systems and all manner of rambling reveries, the poor drupes [fruits having an outer flesh and an inner stone such as cherries] and berries I find in my basket after aimless rambles in woods and pastures." The aimlessness and lack of system were part of the point, which was to preserve things just as they came to him, without second thoughts, without fitting them into predetermined niches. This fidelity to the first blush of an idea or a perception makes Emerson's journals true records of his actual days.

Practical Hints

We do not usually think of Emerson as an intensely practical person. Give us Emerson for ideas, perhaps, but Thoreau for the practical application. But this is to ignore a side of Emerson that is enormously practical, even though the practicality may be masked by humor or drawn out—by fine attention to detail—into astonishing Platonic universals. Once when a wagonload of firewood arrived at Emerson's Concord home while he was indoors talking with his usual gaggle of idealist friends, Emerson looked out the window and, rising from his chair, said, "we must deal with this just as if it were real."

Tide mills were another common reality in Emerson's day. In Boston a dam was built between two points of land jutting out into Massachusetts Bay, and a tide mill was then situated in the middle of the dam to take advantage of the seven- to nine-foot tides in the area. The incoming and outgoing tides turned a waterwheel that ground corn. Emerson admired the skill behind the arrangement "which thus engages the assistance of the moon, like a hired hand, to grind, and wind, and pump, and saw, and split stone, and roll iron." It was just a short step for Emerson to turn this observation into a good phrase: "hitch your wagon to a star [emphasis on the word *your*]." What looks at first like barn-dance exuberance from the Polonius of Concord turns out, on closer examination, to be a happy phrase for a common practical contrivance. This unlikely combination of the high-flying and the down-to-earth is pure Emerson.

The same qualities show up in his advice—almost always in the hortatory mode—about the practical business of writing. Underneath the well-constructed phrase ("I am a rocket-manufacturer," he once remarked) lie the practical demands of the daily struggle for adequate expression.

The best single bit of practical advice about writing Emerson ever gave—best because it is a cry from the heart, because it focuses on attitude not aptitude, and because it is as stirring as a rebel yell—is this: "The way to write is to throw your body at the mark when your arrows are spent."

There is a strangely appealing air of desperation, finality, of terminal urgency to many of Emerson's observations. They come to us as ultimatums, messages found in bottles, fire alarms, battle flags, treasure maps, last words, or family secrets. The poor commentator yearns for boldface, italics, or capital letters: "The only path of escape known in all the worlds of God is performance. You must do your work before you shall be released." Emerson gets the same energy, the same compression, the same authority, when he speaks of "the great class, they who affect our imagination, the men who could not make their hands meet around their objects, the rapt, the lost, the fools of ideas."

Emerson's practical writing advice grows from his personal experience. He spent a great deal of his life preparing to write, trying to write, even writing. In every admonition we hear his willingness to confront his own failures; indeed, he never seems more than a few inches from utter calamity. He urges us to try anything—strategies, tricks, makeshifts. And he always seems to be speaking not only of the nuts and bolts of writing, but of the grain and sinew of his—and our—determination. Sometimes he is terribly direct. If you want to write, just write. "There is no way to learn to write except by writing," he told Woodbury. Sometimes he would just sit down and start writing—anything—to see whether something would happen. He was quick to spot the same trick in others. "I have read," he noted, "that [Richard Brinsley] Sheridan made a good deal of experimental writing with a view to take what might fall, if any wit should transpire in all the waste of pages."

He has little to say about planning, but much about other aspects of getting started. "You should start," he told his young friend, "with no skeleton or plan. The natural one will grow as you work. Knock away all scaffolding. Neither have exordium or peroration. What is it you are writing for anyway? Because you have something new to say? It is the test of the universities and I am glad you have made it yours." This is called free-writing now and is widely used in English composition classes. This is also Coleridge's notion of organic form, which he opposed to the idea of mechanic form. A pear taking shape on the tree is an instance of organic form, while a bowl made by a potter on a wheel is an example of mechanic form. If this attitude leads to an undervaluing of results or products, it leads to a prizing of process, and it is the process of writing that Emerson is particularly good at describing. Speaking about the moment when the general design and possible shape of a piece of writing first occur, Emerson writes, "it is one of the laws of composition that, let the preparation have been however elaborate, how extended so-ever, the moment of casting is yet not less critical, nor the less all-important moment on which the whole success depends." Later he was able to get this down more succinctly: "In writing, the casting moment is of greatest importance, just as it avails not in Daguerre portraits that you have the very man before you, if his expression has escaped." It is no small matter first to recognize the casting moment when you see it, and to keep it in its original form, uncontaminated by later improvements and subtleties and qualifications. Emerson was after the same point when he said, with a Cyrano de Bergerac flash: "Three or four stubborn necessary words are the pith and fate of the business; all the rest is expatiating and qualifying; three or four real choices, acts of will of somebody, the rest is circumstance, satellite, and flourish."

Nature

The practical, down-to-earth Emerson urges us, as we might have guessed, to look to nature for language. On this subject he once quoted Goethe, even though it meant a tussle with German syntax: "They say much of the study of the ancients but what else does that signify, than, direct your attention to the real world, and seek to express it, *since that did* the ancients while they lived." This is the old classic stoic line. For answers to the question of how to live, you must turn, not to the gods, not to history, not to the state or the family, but to nature. Emerson, however, turns to nature not because he is an obedient stoic, but from a terrible personal urgency, rather like that of Thoreau. Emerson's directness, stripped of adjectives, reminds us why he can be considered a modern prophet without our feeling we should apologize for the word. "Our age is retrospective," he begins his grand little book. "It builds the sepulchres of the fathers. It writes biographies, histories, and criticism. The foregoing generations beheld God and nature face to face; we, through their eyes. Why should not we also enjoy an original relation to the universe? Why should not we have a poetry and philosophy of insight, and not of tradition, and a religion by revelation to us, and not the history of theirs?" This is one of the best passages in all of Emerson, not just because it is so deeply typical of him, but because he has here hit upon a fundamental, evergreen view of the world, a way of looking at life available equally to me and to Marcus Aurelius. Simone Weil takes the same way when she urges each of us to escape "the contagion of folly and collective frenzy by reaffirming on his own account, over the head of the social idol, the original pact between the mind and the universe."

In the fourth chapter of *Nature*, a short chapter in a short book, Emerson considers nature as the source of the language with which we grasp the universe and negotiate the mind's pact with it. "Nature is the vehicle of thought," he says, "and in a simple, double, and three fold degree." He then leads the reader in by steps:

1. Words are signs of natural facts.
2. Particular natural facts are symbols of particular spiritual facts.
3. Nature is the symbol of spirit.

The first step is easy. "Words are signs of natural facts. . . . The use of the outer creation [is] to give us language for the beings and changes of the inner creation. Every word which is used to express a moral or intellectual fact, if traced to its root, is found to be borrowed from some material appearance. *Right* means *straight*. *Wrong* means *twisted*. *Spirit* primarily means *wind, transgression* the crossing of a *line; supercilious*, the *raising of the eyebrow*." (In Latin *super* means *raised* and *cilia* means *eyebrow*.) The abstract and vague word *consider* leaps to life when we learn that it originally meant *study the stars.* (In Latin *sidus, sideris* means *star.*) Emerson's recognition of the dependence of language upon nature will lead him, in his 1844 essay "The Poet," to one of the founding insights of the *Oxford English Dictionary*, the dictionary dedicated not to authoritative prescriptions of what English words must mean, but to presenting, through quotations, a short history of every word, showing how it has actually been used. "The poets made all the words," says Emerson, "and therefore language is the archives of history, and, if we must say it, a sort of tomb of the muses. For though the origin of most of our words is forgotten, each word was at first a stroke of genius, and obtained currency because for the moment it symbolized the world to the first speaker and to the hearer. The etymologist finds the deadest word to have been once a brilliant picture. Language is fossil poetry." It is the poet's, the writer's job to "re-attach things to nature." "Genius," says Emerson, "is the activity which repairs the decays of things."

It is rare for Emerson to attack anyone, let alone someone trying to be a writer, but his passion for the best over the second best and his zeal for what he saw as the real world of poetry (which he once called "the science of the real") led him, in *Nature,* to point out that "hundreds of writers may be found in every long-civilized nation, who for a short time believe, and make others believe, that they see and utter truths, who do not of themselves clothe one thought in its natural garment, but who feed unconsciously on the language created by the primary writers of the country, those namely, who hold primarily on nature." It is the true poet— the genius—who can "pierce this rotten diction and fasten words again to visible things."

So far so good. The idea that words are signs of natural facts and that great writers reattach words to their lost or forgotten facts is an idea we entertain willingly. But the next step takes us out in water over our heads. When Emerson says, "Particular natural facts are symbols of particular spiritual facts," he seems to be saying the same sort of thing Carl Jung would say when he observed that the reason daylight and dark night seem so meaningful to us is because light symbolizes knowledge and darkness ignorance to all humans. This is more than just giving a psychological turn to the question; it is, at least in Emerson, a full-court Neoplatonic press. "The world is emblematic. Parts of speech are metaphors, because the whole of nature is a metaphor of the human mind. The laws of moral nature answer to those of matter as face to face in a glass. The visible world and the relation of its parts, is the dial plate of the invisible." For the great Neoplatonic thinkers, "mind is the active force in the universe and matter the passive." This is what lies behind the notion that in Platonism, ideas alone are real and the phenomenal world is a set of copies or appearances. Emerson's assertion that the visible world is the dial plate of the invisible is also a full-dress version of Christian Platonism. Here, by way of illustration and explanation both, is C. S. Lewis's striking distinction between allegory and symbolism. In allegory, as for example in the medieval morality play *Mankind*, we find characters called Naught, New-Guise, and Nowadays. Lewis says,

> if our passions, being immaterial, can be copied by material inventions, then it is possible that our material world in its turn is a copy of an invisible world. . . . The attempt to read that something else through its sensible imitations, to see the archetype in the copy, is what I mean by symbolism or sacramentalism. . . . The allegorist leaves the given—his own passions—to talk of that which is

confessedly less real, which is a fiction. The symbolist leaves the given to find that which is more real. To put the difference another way, for the symbolist it is we who are the allegory.

For anyone able to accept this view—and it is the royal road to Emerson—it becomes a complete worldview. For those who cannot, or cannot yet accept this view as a complete and satisfying metaphysic, it remains a vigorous and valid description of how *writers* use the world of appearances. Emerson's American scholar—and by *scholar* he means pretty much what we mean by *writer*—"shall see that nature is the [mirror image] of the soul, answering to it part for part. One is seal and one is print. Its beauty is the beauty of his own mind. Its laws are the laws of his own mind. Nature then becomes to him the measure of his attainments. So much of nature as he is ignorant of, so much of his own mind does he not yet possess. And in fine the ancient precept 'Know thyself' and the modern precept 'Study nature' become at last one maxim."

"The Universe is the externisation of the soul," says Emerson. This is literally true for the writer. When Theodore Dreiser's Clyde Griffiths first drives to Big Bittern Lake in *An American Tragedy*, Clyde's subconscious has just begun to consider how he might get rid of the cloying—and now pregnant—working girl Roberta, leaving him free to pursue the rich and beautiful Sondra. Dreiser has Clyde

> most strangely impressed at moments and in spots by
> the desolate and for the most part lonely character of the
> region. The narrow and rain-washed and even rutted
> nature of the dirt roads that wound between tall, silent

and darksome trees—forests in the largest sense of the word—that extended for miles and miles apparently on either hand. The decadent and weird nature of some of the bogs and tarns on either side of the only comparatively passable dirt roads which here and there were festooned with funereal or viperous vines, and strewn like deserted battlefields with soggy and decayed piles of fallen and criss-crossed logs—in places as many as four deep—one above the other—in the green slime that an undrained depression in the earth had accumulated.

Dreiser's description of the natural setting clearly mirrors Clyde's state of mind at the time. The lake is where Clyde will bring Roberta and where she will drown when she falls out of the rowboat into the water and Clyde fails to swim to her aid.

To uncloak this angle of vision, to see the relationship between mind and world without the religious language of a Lewis or an Emerson, we must turn to a Dreiser or to Marcel Proust, who takes up the subject again and again. In an early work, *Contre Sainte Beuve*, Proust writes: "What intellect restores to us under the name of the past is not the past. In reality, as soon as each hour of one's life has died, it embodies itself in some material object, as do the souls of the dead in certain folk-stories, and hides there. There it remains captive, captive forever unless we should happen on the object, recognize what lies within, call it by its name, and so set it free." This is why Emerson insists that the poet is not so much a *maker* as a *namer*, and the function of the poet is to be free and to make free.

More Practical Hints

"A Plotinus-Montaigne" was what James Russell Lowell called Emerson, and the description has stuck, suggesting that there are two Emersons—one transcendental and idealistic, the other pragmatic and practical. The Plotinus side, the side that is sure that mind alone is real, and sure of both Primal and Eventual Unity, is limited, as Emerson said Plotinus himself was limited, by being interested only in philosophy. The Montaigne side is seemingly interested in everything but sure of nothing. "Over his name," Emerson tells us, "he drew an emblematic pair of scales and wrote 'Que scais-je?' [what do I know] under it." But it is Montaigne's writing as much as his knowing that interests Emerson. "The sincerity and marrow of the man reaches to his sentences. I know not anywhere the book that seems less written. It is the language of conversation transferred to a book. Cut these words and they would bleed; they are vascular and alive."

Emerson liked Francis Bacon for similar qualities. Some of the similarities are because Emerson's Montaigne is the late-seventeenth-century Charles Cotton translation, done not long after the time of Bacon. "All rising to great place is by a winding stair," says Bacon. "Men of age," he says in another essay, "object too much, consult too long, adventure too little, and repent too soon." Like Emerson, Bacon was drawn to youth. "Young men," he says, "are fitter to invent than judge, fitter for execution than counsel, and fitter for new projects than for settled business." In his Bacon-Montaigne mood, Emerson is darkly eloquent, holding out just enough optimism to avoid complete despair. His essay on Montaigne concludes: "Things seem to tend downward, to justify despondency, to promote rogues, to defeat the just; and by knaves as by martyrs, the just cause is carried forward. Although knaves win in every political struggle, although society seems to be delivered over from the hands of one set of criminals into the hands of another set of criminals, as fast as the government is changed, and the march of civilization is a train of felonies, yet"—and here he finally turns—"yet, general ends are somehow answered."

Each of these sides of Emerson—the Plotinus and the Montaigne-Bacon—requires the other side. The highest goals or ambitions are inevitably judged by whether or not one can take concrete, measurable steps to reach them, while the practical, workaday side of things is most interesting to Emerson when it serves or leads to something great. Emerson is always interested both in what his sentences are aiming for and in the mechanics of the sentences themselves. The words of even the best advice are lifeless unless they have some yeast, some energy in them to get up off the page into the mind.

The positive degree is the sinew of speech, the superlative
    is the fat. . . . When at a trattoria in Florence I asked the
    waiter if the cream was good, the man replied, "Si Signor,
    stupendo."

Avoid adjectives. Let the noun do the work.

It is the best part of each writer which has nothing private in it.

Language should aim to describe the fact, and not merely suggest it.

Art lies not in making your object prominent, but in choosing objects that are prominent.

When he read, Emerson was always on the lookout for what it could teach him about writing. He noted a useful definition for a good style one day: "Nothing can be added to it, neither can anything be taken from it." He then gave as an example an epitaph of a "criminal who was killed by a fall from his horse" which he found in Boswell's *Johnson*.

> Between the stirrup and the ground
> I mercy asked, I mercy found.

Emerson's comment is "which word can you spare? What word can you add?" Though Emerson may seem learned and bookish—we only come upon him in books—he is always looking for a way to break free and do something fresh. Listening one day to the local minister in Concord, Emerson observed how he "grinds and grinds in the mill of a truism and nothing comes out but what was put in. But the moment he or I desert the tradition and speak a spontaneous thought, instantly poetry, wit, hope, virtue, learning and anecdote, all flock to our aid."

If Emerson's writing does not always, or even usually, proceed in a straightforward, logical manner, it is not because he couldn't write that way, but because he didn't want to, and was after something different. "If you desire to arrest attention, to surprise, do not give me the facts in the order of cause and effect, but drop one or two links in the chain, and give me a cause and an effect two or three times removed." His own mention of moon-powered tide mills followed by "hitch your wagon to a star" is an example, as is "An institution is the lengthened shadow of one man." "The most interesting writing," he told Woodbury, "is that which does not quite satisfy the reader. Try and leave a little thinking for him. . . . A little guessing does him no harm, so I would assist him with no connections. If you can see how the harness fits, he can. But make sure that you see it."

Coherence, then, is something that happens in the reader's mind. Here, as in so many places, Emerson is interested in the actual processes of reading and writing, in what would be called a century later the phenomenology of reading and writing, an interest not in what *should* happen, but in what *does* happen. Full coherence in a text, then, for Emerson, was a blemish: "'Do not put hinges to your work to make it cohere,' he once said in substance to me." This is Woodbury talking. "And we must remember that through such joints much sophistry has crept into the world. Sincerity," Woodbury goes on, "was Mr. Emerson's soul and he unhesitatingly preferred lack of continuity to the least ambiguity regarding intention. Classification for the sake of external order and system was unnatural to him."

"Consistency," Emerson famously wrote, "is the hobgoblin of little minds." To Woodbury, Emerson explained why: "Neither concern yourself about consistency. The moment you putty and plaster your expressions to make them hang together, you have begun a weakening process. Take it for granted that the truths will harmonize; and as for the falsities and mistakes, they will speedily die of themselves. If you must be contradictory, let it be clean and sharp as the two blades of scissors meet."

Emerson is always inciting his reader to write it. Here, for example, is one of the outbursts—cries from the heart—that let us suddenly see what it was that Walt Whitman and so many others were responding to: "All writing is by the grace of God. People do not deserve to have good writing, they are so pleased with bad. . . . Give me initiative, spermatic, prophesying, man-making words."

Emerson already knew the importance of attention, the subject to which William James would give so much attention. "The power to detach and to magnify by detaching, is the essence of rhetoric in the hands of the orator and poet," Emerson wrote in "Art." He showed his own preferred mode of focusing a reader's attention when he spoke slightingly of all the "denying, preparing, wondering and quoting" he found in literature, "but of calm affirming, very little." Directness, boldness, going at once to the central point—courage, in a word, was the quality most needed. "He is a poor writer who does not teach courage of treatment."

Emerson's non-Calvinist, Rousseau-like belief that we are born not just good, but open—to the world and to others—led him to prize first thoughts, hints, glimmers, premonitions, first-formings, harbingers, and he took extraordinary care all his life to capture in writing his first impressions. He told Elizabeth Peabody to write down her thoughts *as they came to her*, and in the imagery *in which they first appeared*. He did this himself, and he was even careful to write down what he could remember of his dreams when he awoke. Some of Emerson's best things come from his dreams and from his hunger to capture them. In 1840, with *Nature*, "The American Scholar," and "The Divinity School Address" behind him;

with the Brook Farm experiment on his horizon; with his children flourishing, his marriage solid, and his friendship with Margaret Fuller ripening, Emerson, now in his late thirties, was full of energy and confidence in what he called "these flying days." "I dreamed," he wrote in his journal, "that I floated at will in the great ether, and I saw this world floating also not far off, but diminished to the size of an apple. Then an angel took it in his hand and brought it to me and said, 'this must thou eat.' And I ate the world."

This startling image, of a sort of global Eucharist, which Emerson caught out of a dream before it could dissolve, is a New World apple story, a mythogenetic moment that can stand with the stories of Adam and Eve, Atalanta, and Isaac Newton.

What he valued for himself he valued in others. When he became editor of *The Dial*, he made room in the magazine for a new department (he called it "Verses of the Portfolio") which would present emerging work, work not yet fixed or final or ready for conventional publication. The first poet whose initial lunge at a draft was thus made public was Ellery Channing. Emerson could quite calmly publish work that was not yet publishable because he was sure that process mattered more than product, that the act of writing was more important than the written and finished piece. "Power ceases," he once wrote—splendidly—"in the instant of repose; it resides in the moment of transition from a past to a new state, in the shooting of the gulf, in the darting to an aim. This one fact the world hates; that the soul becomes." Form for Emerson is always secondary, always provisional, always only in the service of the emerging thought. "For the best part . . . of every mind is not that which he knows, but that which hovers in gleams, suggestions, tantalizing unpossessed before him. His firm recorded knowledge soon loses all interest for him. But this dancing chorus of thoughts and hopes is the quarry of his future, is his possibility."

We expect unlimited optimism from such a committed attention to the process of writing in preference to the finished product, but Emerson's attention to process included a vivid and chagrined awareness of the weaknesses, misses, and failures that so often dog the efforts of anyone who writes. "I lose days," he noted merrily, "determining how hours should be spent." He loved—who does not?—Samuel Johnson's last-ditch heave of will. "I soon found," says Johnson in the preface to his *Dictionary*, "that it is too late to look for instruments when the work calls for execution, and that whatever abilities I had brought to my task, with those I must finally perform it." In his own case, and he didn't try to spare or excuse himself, Emerson noted the endless velvet alternatives to hard work. "Always that work is more pleasant to the imagination which is not now required."

One reason Emerson still speaks to the modern writer is just this awareness of the failures, doubts, inadequacies, evasions, of the many times and reasons when the work grows cold. He seems always to be doing less than his best, something other than his real work. "In my memoirs I must record that I always find myself doing something less than my best task. In the spring I was writing politics; now I am writing a biography, which not the absolute command, but facility and amiable feeling prompted." He lived with, acknowledged, and named cramp, mildew, utter inglorious collapse, and the terrible power of mere mood. "Our moods do not believe in each other. Today I am full of thoughts and can write what I please. I see no reason why I should not have the same thought, the same power of expression tomorrow. What I write, whilst I write it, seems the most natural thing in the world; but yesterday I saw a dreary vacuity in this direction in which I now see so much; and a month hence I doubt not, I shall wonder who he was that wrote so many continuous pages."

Some sheer need for expression—no matter what—drove him on. When he had nothing to say, he wrote about having nothing to say. "Since I came home I do not write much and writing is always my metre of health—writing, which a sane philosopher would probably say was the surest symptom of a diseased mind." When the writing went poorly, he didn't pretend otherwise. "When I write a letter to anyone whom I love, I have no lack of words or thoughts; I am wiser than myself and [read] my paper with the pleasure of one who received a letter, but what I write to fill the gaps of a chapter is hard and cold, is grammar and logic; there is no magic in it; I do not wish to see it again."

This emphasis—bordering on overemphasis—on failure, is redeemed for us, as it probably was for Emerson, by humor. He seems always to see the funny side of insufficiency. "A man can only write one book. That is the reason why everyone begs readings and extracts of the young poet until 35. When he is 50, they still think they value him, and tell him so, but they scatter like partridges if he offer to read his paper."

In *Representative Men*, Emerson ended each of his biographical sketches with a paragraph or so on the shortcomings of the person he was writing about. Thus Plato, he says, is too literary and his work lacks "the vital authority which the screams of prophets and the sermons of unlettered Arabs and Jews possess." Napoleon, for all his military genius, "left France smaller, poorer, feebler than he found it, and the whole contest for freedom was to be begun again." For any excellence there was a compensating offset, writers being no exception.

It is easy to hide for something,—to hide now, that we may draw the more admiration anon. Easy to sit in the shade, if we have a Plato's Republic teeming in the brain, which will presently be born for the joy and illumination of men. . . . But how if you have no security of such a result; how if the fruit of your brain is abortive, if cramp and mildew, if dreams and the songs of dreams, if prose and crochets and cold trifles, matter unreadable by other men and odious to your own eyes be the issue? How if you must sit out the day in thoughtful attitude and experiment, and return to the necessities and conversation of the household without the support of any product, and they must believe you and you may doubt that this waste can be justified?

Unwilling to conclude on this gloomy note, and for once seeing no humor in it, Emerson falls back on formulaic optimism, but we can tell by his whistling that he is passing a graveyard. "I call you to a confidence which surmounts this painful experience" he goes soldiering on. "You are to have a selfsupport which maintains you not only against all others, but against your own skepticism. . . . The Saharas must be crossed as well as the Nile. It is easy to live for others; every body does. I call on you to live for yourselves, so shall you find in this penury and absence of thought, a purer splendor than ever clothed the exhibitions of wit."

Emerson wrote rapidly, so rapidly that the ink often wasn't dry when he turned over a page, but he did not write easily. He felt assailed by endless disincentives to write. His strategy was not to paper over the problems, but to drag them into full sun, with humor if he could, without it if he must. The essential thing was to try again. He noted how parents watch their children get knocked down or set back and how these same parents learn to pray for their children's resilience. It's not the setback that matters, it's what happens next. Sometimes Emerson compared himself and his contemporaries to the great Persian poets:

"Loose the knot of the heart," says Hafiz. At the Opera, I think I see the fine gates open which are at all times closed, and tomorrow I shall find free and varied expression. But tomorrow I am as mute as yesterday. Expression is all we want: Not knowledge, but vent: we know enough, but have not leaves and lungs enough for a healthy perspiration and growth. Hafiz has; Hafiz's good things, like those of all good poets, are the cheap blessings of water, air and fire. [Or t]he observations, analogies, and felicities which arise so profusely in writing a letter to a friend. An air of sterility, poor, thin, arid, reluctant vegetation belongs to the wise and unwise whom I know. If they have fine traits, admirable traits, they have a palsied side. But an utterance whole, generous, sustained, equal, graduated-at-will, such as Montaigne, such as Beaumont and Fletcher so easily and habitually sustain, I miss in myself most of all, but also in my contemporaries. A palace style of manners and conversation, to which every morrow is a new day, which exists extempore and is equal to the needs of life, at once tender and bold, and with great arteries like Cleopatra or Corinne, would be satisfying, and we should be willing to die when our time came, having had our swing and gratification. But my fine souls are cautious and canny, and wish to unite Corinth with Connecticut. I see no easy help for it.

And indeed there is no easy help for it. We need the power to write, but that is only the beginning. We also need the resilience to rebound from our setbacks, the willingness to finish what we start, and the strength to hold out for performance over intention. Emerson casts these concerns as practical matters for the working writer; the qualities required are all forms of power, talismans for the pragmatist who evaluates things by their fruits, not their roots. Of course we want to know the sources of power. We die for lack of such knowledge. "My heart's inquiry," said Emerson, "is, whence is your power?" And, "The one thing we want to know is where is power to be bought. [We would give any price] for condensation, concentration, and the recalling at will high mental energy." But the real question is always what can you *do* with the powers you do in fact have. The only acceptable answer for Emerson is performance. "I value men as they can complete their creation. One man can hurl from him a sentence which is spheral, and at once and forever disengaged from the author. Another can say excellent things, if the sayer and the circumstance are known and considered; but the sentences need a running commentary, and are not yet independent individuals that can go alone."

The Language of the Street

Emerson pointedly preferred the language of the street and of action to that of the study. "Life is our dictionary," he says in "The American Scholar."

> Years are well spent in country labors; in town; in the insight into trades and manufactures; in frank intercourse with many men and women; in science; in art; to the one end of mastering in all their facts a language by which to illustrate and embody our perceptions. I learn immediately from any speaker how much he has already lived, through the poverty or splendor of his speech. Life lies behind us as the quarry from whence we get tiles and copestones for the masonry of today. This is the way to learn grammar. Colleges and books only copy the language which the field and the work-yard made.

It was a subject he warmed to again and again. "I ask not for the great, the remote, the romantic; what is doing in Italy or Arabia. . . . I embrace the common, I explore and sit at the feet of the familiar, the low. Give me insight into today, and you may have the antique and future worlds. What would we really know the meaning of? The meal in the firkin; the milk in the pan; the ballad in the street; the news of the boat; the glance of the eye; the form and gait of the body."

Emerson did not always succeed in his language, and his street is not our street. People where I live eat out of a lunchbox or a to-go box, not a firkin. But Emerson's democratic leanings were always inclining him toward plain, or as we might say, accessible, language. Questions about the public good, he thought, "should not be addressed to the imagination or to our literary associations, but to the ear of plain men [in language] such as plain men, farmers, mechanics, teamsters, seamen or soldiers—might offer, if they would gravely, patiently, humbly reflect upon the matter. There is nothing in their want of book-learning to hinder. This doctrine affirms that there is imparted to every man the Divine light of reason sufficient not only to plant corn and grind wheat by but also to illuminate all his life his social, political, religious actions. . . . Every man's reason is sufficient for his guidance, *if used*."

Emerson was interested not just in common language but in the spoken language. His essays all began as lectures. His writing was first speaking. He noted that his friend Thomas Carlyle "has seen as no other in our time how inexhaustible a mine is the language of conversation. He does not use the *written* dialect of the time in which scholars, pamphleteers, and the clergy write, not the parliamentary dialect, in which the lawyer, the statesman, and the better newspapers write, but draws strength and motherwit out of a poetic use of the *spoken* vocabulary, so that his paragraphs are all a sort of splendid conversation." Emerson's long correspondence with Carlyle was one such conversation, and Emerson set its value high. "Strict conversation with a friend is the magazine out of which all good writing is drawn."

Not that Carlyle's own writing was entirely beyond criticism. In one letter, after praising Carlyle's *The French Revolution* effusively and at length, Emerson added: "I will tell you more of the book when I have once got it at focal distance—if that can ever be, and muster my objections when I am sure of their ground. I insist, of course, that it might be more simple, less Gothically efflorescent. You will say no rules for the illumination of windows can apply to the aurora borealis. However I find refreshment when every now and then a special fact slips into the narrative couched in sharp business-like terms."

Though Emerson spent much of his working life in his ground floor study in the house in Concord, the room behind the crude but vigorous color print of Vesuvius erupting in 1794 that hung beside the entrance to the study, he was—as the picture perhaps hints—acutely aware of the pitfalls of the sequestered life, and he struggled to stay in touch with the great outer working world. "Now and then a man exquisitely made can and must live alone; but coop up most men, and you undo them. The king lived and [ate] in hall, with men, and understood men; said Selden. 'Read Law?' said Jeremiah Mason. ''Tis in the courtroom you must read law.' And I say if you would learn to write, 'tis in the street, in the street."

And just as he insists on self-trust and going it alone, he never lost sight of the fact that language has its broad base in the people. "The plain style indicates that the people had their share in it." Yet this recognition of the strength of plain popular language did not lead him, as it led so many of his friends, into the Utopian conviction that the New World writer must labor in the fields or the factory all day like everyone else, and then go home and write after the day's real work. "Tell children what you say about writing and laboring with the hands," he fumed in his journal.

> I know better. Can you distill rum by minding it at odd times? Or analyse soils? Or carry on the Suffolk Bank? Or the Greenwich Observatory? Or sail a ship through the narrows by minding the helm when you happen to think of it? Or serve a glass house, or a steam-engine, or a telegraph, or a railroad express? Or accomplish anything good or anything powerful in this manner? Nothing whatever. And the greatest of all arts, the subtlest, and of most miraculous effect you fancy is to be practiced with a pen in one hand and a crowbar or a peat-knife in the other. . . . A writer must live and die by his writing. Good for that and good for nothing else. A War; an earthquake, the revival of letters, the new dispensation by Jesus, or by Angels, Heaven, Hell, power, science, the Neant [Nothingness],—exist only to him as colors for his brush. That you think he can write at odd minutes only shows what your knowledge of writing is.

Then Emerson adds, with a flicker of scorn he rarely allows himself, but which shows what he thought of the average writing of his time and place, "American writing can be written at odd minutes,—Unitarian writing, Congress speeches, railroad novels." The language of the street might be Emerson's starting place, or the quarry where he went for language, but he was, from the beginning, aiming at something else.

Words

One modern critic has wondered how Emerson wrote as well as he did, considering how little faith he had in words as such. It is an empty judgment. Emerson loved language as much as any poet does, but he understood that reality is larger than language. If you call a dog's tail a leg, how many legs does the dog have? The answer is four. Calling a tail a leg does not make it one. "All language," says Emerson in "The Poet," "is vehicular and transitive, and is good, as horses and ferries are, for conveyance, not as farms and houses are, for homestead." Emerson did care for language—a great deal—but he always insisted that words do not exist as things in themselves, but *stand for things* which are finally more real than the words. This means taking even more care with one's choice of words. "Skill in writing," he says flatly, "consists in making every word cover a thing." He was always alert for what happens when we forget this. "Scholars," he says, "are found to make very shabby sentences out of the weakest words because of exclusive attention to the word." A writer needs to get in as close as possible to the thing itself. "Chaucer, Milton and Shakespeare have seen mountains, if they speak of them. The young writers seem to have seen pictures of mountains. The wish to write poetry they have, but not the poetic fury; and what they write is studies, sketches, fantasies, and not yet the inestimable poem."

As a philosopher, Emerson favored what philosophers unhelpfully call realism, which is the belief that ideas alone are real. As a writer, though, the Montaigne side of Emerson comes uppermost, and he becomes our kind of realist, a person who believes that there is a real world out there, however imperfectly we perceive it. Since the world is real, the words chosen to describe it must be chosen with all possible care; language reform consists largely of reattaching words to things, and, in the process, redeeming the things and recharging the language. "There is every degree of remoteness from the line of things in the line of words. By and by comes a word true and closely embracing the thing. That is not Latin nor English nor any language, but thought. The aim of the author is not to tell the truth—that he cannot do, but to suggest it. He has only approximated it himself, and hence his cumbrous embarrassed speech: he uses many words, hoping that one, and not another, will bring you as near to the fact as he is."

Emerson fought the use of abstractions. "I cannot hear a sermon without being struck by the fact that amid the drowsy series of sentences what a sensation a historical fact, a biographical name, a sharply objective illustration makes! Why will not the preacher heed the momentary silence of his congregation and [realize] that this particular sentence is all they carry away? Only in a purely scientific composition which by its text and structure addresses itself to philosophers is a writer at liberty to use mere abstractions." The best words will deliver the thing behind the words. "The true conciseness of style would be such a writing as no dictionaries but events and character only could illustrate." He liked George Fox for saying, "What I am in words, I am the same in life."

Abstraction writ large is Tradition.

If I were called upon to charge a minister, I would say beware of Tradition: Tradition which embarrasses life and falsifies all teaching. The sermons that I hear are all dead of that ail. The preacher is betrayed by his ear. He begins to inveigh against some real evils and falls unconsciously into formulas of speech which have been said and sung in the church some ages and have lost all life. They never had any but when freshly and with special conviction applied. But you must never lose sight of the purpose of helping a particular person in every word you say.

Of course the same thing applies not just to the church and to sermons, but to all writing and speaking, to all activity where it is a matter of how you choose to use words. It is not enough to understand the importance of words; you must be able to use them yourself. "The art of writing consists in putting two things together that are unlike and that belong together like a horse and cart. Then have we somewhat far more goodly and efficient than either."

Choosing words and using words are the central inescapable acts of writing. "No man can write well who thinks there is any choice of words for him. [By choice here Emerson means a group of acceptable words, any one of which he could choose.] The laws of composition are as strict as those of sculpture and architecture. There is always one right line that ought to be drawn or one proportion that should be kept and every other line or proportion is wrong. . . . So in writing, there is always a right word, and every other that is wrong."

The control and placement of emphasis are partly a question of sentence mechanics and partly a matter of word choice. In a wonderfully titled book that Melville also read and cited,

Guesses at Truth by the Hare brothers, Emerson found this: "In good prose, (says Schlegel) every word should be underlined . . . No italics in Plato . . . In good writing every word means something. In good writing words become one with things."

Emerson seems to have followed one rule of thumb much of the time—though I cannot find it stated explicitly anywhere—and that is: where you can, use words of one syllable. The English language from the Renaissance on has a sort of genius for monosyllables. So Emerson can say "never read any book that is not a year old," in which even the polysyllabic words seem monosyllabic. In his best work, monosyllabic words set the tone. A journal entry for 1855 reads, "If a man has good corn, or wood, or boards, or pigs to sell, or can make better chairs, or knives, crucibles or church organs than anybody else, you will find a broad, hard-beaten road to his house, though it be in the woods."

Emerson's advice gains traction with us by his advice not just on what to use, but on what to avoid. Writers should avoid abstractions and Latinisms and use short, concrete Anglo-Saxon or Germanic words. They should also be wary of overused words. "If I made laws for Shakers or a School," said Emerson, "I should gazette [forbid] every Saturday all the words they were wont to use in reporting religious experience as 'Spiritual life,' 'God,' 'soul,' 'cross,' etc and if they could not find new ones next week they might remain silent." Elsewhere in his journal he drew up a list of gazetted terms: "'after all,' 'Kindred Spirit,' 'yes, to a certain extent,' 'as a general thing,' and 'quite a number.'"

Finally, though, writers must add or subtract what they can, but they must save the intuition. For after all, Emerson insists, "Literature is a heap of nouns and verbs enclosing an intuition or two."

Sentences

Words are the writer's clay; the sentence is the writer's brick-mold. For Emerson the sentence—not the paragraph and not the essay—is the main structural and formal unit. This was a deliberate, self-conscious matter. He was endlessly curious about sentence mechanics, and he combed his reading for examples of good sentences. He knew that the sentence is the basic unit of prose and he talked about the subject frequently.

The maker of a sentence like the other artist launches out into the infinite and builds a road into Chaos and old Night.

Whosoever . . . apprehends the infinite, and every man can, brings all worth and significance into that spot of space where he stands though it be a ditch, a potato-field, a work bench. . . . And therefore also is it that every good sentence seems to imply all truth.

My debt to Plato is a certain number of sentences: the like to Aristotle. A large number, yet still a finite number, make the worth of Milton and Shakespeare, to me. I would therefore run over what I have written, save out the good sentences, and destroy the rest.

He only is a good writer who keeps one eye on his page and with the other sweeps over things. So that every new sentence brings us a new contribution of observation.

[Carlyle] believes that every noble nature was made by God, and contains—if savage passions—also fit checks and grand impulses within it, hath its own resources, and, however erring, will return from afar. Then he writes English and crowds meaning into all the nooks and corners of his sentences. Once read he is but half read.

Two proverbs I found lately; one; "He who would bring home the wealth of the Indies, must carry out the wealth of the Indies." The other may serve as a foil to this magnificent sentence, "Small pot, soon hot." Then again I found in "The Phenix" the Persian sentence "Remember always that the gods are good," which for genius equals any other golden saying.

Emerson's lifelong interest in sentences pushed him toward epigram and proverb, and steered him away from narrative, from logic, from continuity, from formal arrangement and effect. Pushed as far as he pushed them, many of Emerson's sentences stand out by themselves, alone and exposed like scarecrows in a cornfield, an effect he was painfully aware of. "Here I sit," he wrote Carlyle, "and read and write with very little system and as far as regards composition with the most fragmentary result: paragraphs incompressible each sentence an infinitely repellent particle." At other times he could compare his sentence-by-sentence method to hopping from stone to stone across a stream: "My thoughts are too short, as they say my sentences are. I step along from stone to stone over the Lethe which gurgles around my path, but the odds are that my companion encounters me just as I leave one stone and before my foot has reached the other and down I tumble into Lethe water."

Sometimes he appears to be clinging to his belief that writing good sentences would be enough, even though he always knew there was more to writing than just writing sentences. "I know not why [Walter Savage] Landor should have so few readers. His book seems to me as original in its form as in its substance. He has no dramatic power, no epic power, but he makes sentences, which though not gravitation and electricity is still vegetation. After twenty years I still read his strange dialogues with pleasure, not only sentences but page after page the whole discourse." At other times his reading turned up rich prose which seemed to mock his own sentence-based work. "[Rabelais'] style at once decides the high quality of the man. It flows like the river Amazon, so rich, so plentiful, so transparent, and with such long reaches, that longanimity or longsightedness which belongs to the Platos. No sand without lime, no short chippy indigent epigrammatist or proverbialist with docked sentences but an exhaustless affluence."

When his sentences work, which is often enough, his success can be traced to his taking endless pains with sentence mechanics. He liked sentences that had a little bite or pop, a flash-point, and he had several different ways of achieving this effect, which we may distinguish as the whip-crack, the back-flip, the brass ring (hole in one), and the mousetrap. In the whip-crack sentence, it is the final word that makes the whole sentence snap. "Every man is wanted, but no man is wanted much." In another case, already quoted, it is not the last word but the last phrase that pulls the trigger. "Meek young men grow up in libraries believing it their duty to accept the views which Cicero, which Locke, which Bacon have given, forgetful that Cicero, Locke, and Bacon were only young men in libraries when they wrote those books." Another common device for Emerson is the back-flip, where the energy comes from a pat reversal.

Every hero becomes a bore at last.
Nothing astonishes men so much as common sense and
    plain dealing.
I wish to write such rhymes as shall not suggest restraint,
    but contrariwise the wildest freedom.

Most of his devices put the explosive bit, the verbal energy, at the end of the sentence, much as German prefers to put the verb at the end of the sentence, so that, by a kind of back-wash, the energy floods back through the early part of the sentence.

Sometimes Emerson manages to catch the brass ring and come up with one of the unforgettable phrases that have floated loose in English—sometimes associated with his name, sometimes not—ever since.

All mankind love a lover.
Hitch your wagon to a star.
Here once the embattled farmers stood, / And fired the shot
    heard round the world.
Things are in the saddle, / and ride mankind.
If you write a better book, or preach a better sermon, or
    build a better mousetrap than your neighbor, the world
    will make a beaten path to your door.

And finally, there is the mousetrap sentence, usually baited with a Latinate abstraction, and usually sprung with plain Anglo-Saxon.

A foolish consistency is the hobgoblin of little minds.
An institution is the lengthened shadow of one man.
Our chief want in life is somebody who shall make us do
  what we can.

Emblem, Symbol, Metaphor

If language begins in the street, so do symbols and metaphors. "The schools of poets and philosophers are not more intoxicated with their symbols than the populace with theirs," he says in his 1844 essay "The Poet."

> In our political parties, compute the power of badges and emblems. See the great ball which they roll from Baltimore to Bunker Hill! In the political processions Lowell goes in a loom, and Lynn in a shoe, and Salem in a ship. Witness the cider-barrel, the log-cabin, the hickory stick, the palmetto, and all the cognizances of party. See the power of national emblems. Some stars, lilies, leopards, a crescent, a lion, an eagle or other figure which came into credit God knows how, on an old rag of bunting, blowing in the wind on a fort at the ends of the earth, shall make the blood tingle under the rudest or most conventional exterior. The people fancy they hate poetry, and they are all poets and mystics.

Emerson's fondness for symbol and metaphor—for figurative language—is, of course, more than politics and populism. He personally found figurative language exciting and strangely moving. "The use of symbols," he says in "The Poet," "has a certain power of emancipation and exhilaration for all men. We seem to be touched by a wand which makes us dance and run about happily like children. We are like persons who come out of a cave or cellar into the open air. This is the effect on us of tropes, fables, oracles, and all poetic forms." Emerson would have loved the suggestion of Alistair Reid that when we tire of counting to ten in the same old way, we try new ways, such as "ounce, dice, trice, quartz, quince, sago, serpent, oxygen, nitrogen, denim." I have seen a classroom's worth of bored freshmen light up with broad smiles on hearing this string.

Figurative language delights and exhilarates because it promises more than meets the eye. To paraphrase Emerson's scheme in the "Language" chapter of *Nature*, already touched on above, words stand for things, things stand for ideas, and the world of things stands for the world of ideas. Another way to look at the elevation—the acceleration—in this scheme is Alain Robbe-Grillet's bold prediction, "If you begin by believing in metaphor, you will end by believing in God."

We are here approaching the full sacramental or symbolic view of the world described by C. S. Lewis in *The Allegory of Love*—the view that "in symbolism it is we who are the allegory." "Have mountains, and waves, and skies, no significance but what we consciously give them when we employ them as emblems of our thoughts?" asks Emerson. He goes on, answering himself, "The world is emblematic. Parts of speech are metaphors, because the whole of nature is a metaphor of the human mind. The laws of moral nature answer to those of matter as face to face in a glass. The visible world and the relation of its parts, is the dial plate of the invisible."

Pushed just a little further, this view takes on a religious, or perhaps we should say with Emerson a spiritual, aspect. "A Fact," he says, "is the end or last issue of spirit. The visible creation is the terminus or the circumference of the invisible world." This is, in fact, however we or Emerson may mask it, the full symbolic or sacramental vision of the world. "'Things more excellent than every image,' says Jamblichus, 'are expressed through images.' Things admit of being used as symbols because nature is a symbol, in the whole and in every part." "The Universe is the externalization of the soul," says Emerson, who then puts his finger on the living center. "Wherever the life is, that [the soul] bursts into appearance around it."

The creation of a work of literature mimics the creation of the world, mimics the creativity of God or of Nature. A good deal depends on which words we elect to start with a capital letter. "Good writing and brilliant discourse are perpetual allegories," writes Emerson. "This imagery is spontaneous. It is the blending of experience with the present action of the mind. It is proper creation. It is the working of the Original Cause through the instruments he has already made." Sacramentalism, Platonism, Neoplatonism, Hegelianism, and Christianity are all forms of idealism, and as William Gass has insisted, "The forms of fiction and the aims of art support Idealism, whatever the sentences of any novel assert." Idealism works for the writer. Never mind Creation, for, as Emerson puts it, "it [the imagery of good writing] is proper creation." And if Emerson could swallow the world in a dream, he could also move it around like a slide under a microscope. "The world being thus put under the mind for verb and noun, the poet is he who can articulate it," he says in "The Poet." And it is literary creation Emerson has in mind when he adds, "We are symbols and inhabit symbols; work-men, work, and tools, words and things, birth and death, all are emblems."

A striking modern example of this process is Paul Scott's *Raj Quartet*. In *The Towers of Silence*, which is part three of this magnificent novel about the end of British rule in India, the main character is a retired English missionary school-teacher named Barbie Batchelor, who comes, early in the book, upon Emerson's essay "History." "Barbie emerged with a volume of Emerson still open at the page with her thumb on the line 'man is explicable by nothing less than all his history,' which a moment ago had caused her to catch her breath." She returns to the book as to a guilty pleasure.

> Barbie sat at the writing table, opened the rejected book. "If the whole of history is in one man," she read, "it is all to be explained from individual experience. There is a relation between the hours of our life and the centuries of time." She closed the book abruptly and made herself busy in the room, opening drawers and rearranging their contents.
>
> Not taking Emerson back she returned to him daily like a sparrow easily frightened from a promising scatter-ing of crumbs by the slightest move, with a nagging sense of having more duties than intelligence. . . .
>
> She began to feel what she believed Emerson wanted her to feel; that in her own experience lay an explanation not only of history but of the lives of other people, there-fore an explanation of the things that had happened to Edwina and to Miss Manners of whom she had only the vaguest picture.

Returning still later to Emerson, Barbie reads on: "'Each new law and political movement has meaning for you,' Barbie read and was convinced that this might be so because Emerson told her. 'Stand before each of its tablets and say "here is one of my coverings. Under this fantastic or odious or graceful mask did my Protean nature hide itself." This remedies the defect of our too great nearness to ourselves.'" And yet further on, Barbie finds this: "The world exists for the education of each man."

Emerson's "History" contains the key to Scott's masterpiece. Scott wrote approvingly of the collective conscience which "History" describes, and the essay's idea of history as something that must be individually experienced and explained works perfectly for the serious historical novelist. The point is to see that each life, any life, is emblematic of the whole, of some aspect of the whole. One reads this part of the *Quartet* with the same shock of recognition that Barbie Batchelor felt in her Emerson.

Barbie's life is entwined with the book's other characters until, late in *The Towers of Silence*, Barbie is destroyed by her own past, by the trunks and boxes of her possessions lashed to a runaway cart careening downhill. So it was with the Raj, destroyed by the burden of its past catching up with it. The *Quartet*'s point, Scott's point, Barbie's point, is Emerson's point that each of us is emblematic of the whole, that all of history is to be explained by each life. This is no abstraction.

Audience

Henry James once gave it as his reason for leaving Paris to live in London that in France, in those days, it was impossible for an American to be admitted to the best society, whereas in England James found he was welcome everywhere if he would just take pains to make himself entertaining. I remember being surprised by this information. He was Henry James. Of course people would be interested in him without his raising a finger to make himself interesting. But he did not feel that way. And if Henry James felt he had to exert himself to make himself agreeable or entertaining, what did that say about the rest of us?

What Henry James learned from the social world of dinner parties, Emerson learned early from public speaking. Most of Emerson's writing was done first for delivery as public lecture. This meant that he was always aware of language as spoken language, that he was always mindful of an actual physical, visible audience. He was also aware, early on, that he could not assume that the audience was interested in him when it first filed in and sat down. It was his job, he felt, to earn the attention of the audience. This awareness is vividly illustrated in a letter he wrote when he was twenty-five to his younger brother Charles, who was generally considered the brightest and most promising of the Emerson boys. The letter is written in the third person and is an extended critique of a speech Charles had recently given. Emerson's evaluation of his brother's effort may not have pleased Charles if indeed he ever read it. There is no evidence the letter was sent or delivered to Charles—it isn't even signed—and its significance is not the family relationship so much as the general importance of the relation between speaker and hearer or between writer and reader.

To Charles Chauncy Emerson
15 JULY 1828
This day I heard Mr. C. C. Emerson deliver a valedictory oration to his class. This young man's performance deserves a particular notice. He is a beautiful orator but never eloquent. His advantages for speaking both natural and acquired are very great. His voice, his person and his action are (to that end) excellent. But the vice of his oratory lies here—he is a *spectacle* instead of being an *engine*: a fine show at which we look, instead of an agent that moves us. There is very good management of the voice, fine tones, varied and delicate sounds—some that are music to hear; there is very elegant and very nervous [i.e., sensitive] gesture; and these are used to convey beautiful and forcible periods indeed a very finished oration—to all who have a mind to hear it. There's the rub—you may hear it or not as you choose. The orator leaves you to your option. He does not address you. He has chalked round him a circle on the floor and within that he exhibits these various excellences to all the curious. I happened to see

the manuscript before it was pronounced, and noted
a particular passage which was a sudden and touch-
ing appeal to the audience with the remark that Mr. E
would not speak it well. It was even so. Though he uttered
the words, *he did not appeal* to the audience. And so
that moving passage passed with no more effect than
if the same elegant speaker had said butterfly, butterfly,
butterfly.—In short during this very pleasing performance
I was many times reminded of Mr. Everett's remark upon
the ancients that they made the greatest advances in arts
and commerce and politics and yet in each, through some
strange mischance, fell short of the last advance. So Mr. E.
with noble elements for eloquence, was all but eloquent.
I felt that that voice should have thrilled me as a trumpet.
I only heard it with pleasure. I felt that he should have
made me laugh and cry at his will. He never touched me.

The cause of this peculiarity in this gentleman's
harangue appeared to me to be that he has come with a
wrong feeling to the rostrum. His rank in College is very
high. He has long enjoyed a considerable reputation for
talents and acquirements and particularly as a speaker.
The whole audience were known to him and were drawn
together by the expectation of witnessing his powers.
Mr. E was fully aware of all this, and aware that whatever he said would be eagerly and favorably listened to.
Instead, therefore, of feeling that the audience was an
object of attention from him, he felt that he was an object
of attention to the audience. This of course is the reverse
of what it should be. Instead of finding his audience—like
other orators—an angry master who is to be pacified, or
a sturdy master who is to be cajoled,—and in any case,
one whose difficult regard is to be won,—he takes it for

granted that he has the command. He makes a *King's Speech*; condescendingly drops very fine things, which, if you listen with all your might, will pay you.

As Revolutions take place in Colleges as well as monarchies, it appears that Mr. E.'s situation is changed. He has been removed with some violence from the first to the second place. I suppose this event will do more than all masters or instructions, to mend the great error I have remarked—to push him out of his enchanted circle. He no longer claims deference by an unbroken prescription. His best title has been formally denied. At his next public appearance, he is to struggle uphill; he is to vindicate a right which has been set aside. Let him feel his situation. Let him remember that the true orator must not wrap himself in himself, but must wholly abandon himself to the sentiment he utters and to the multitude he addresses;—must become their property, to the end that *they may become his*. Like Pericles, let him "thunder and lighten." Let him for a moment forget himself, and then, assuredly, he will not be forgotten.

Emerson had obviously already learned all this for himself, and he rarely lost sight of his intended audience in later life. The subject crops up over and over in his journals. "If I could persuade men to listen to their interior convictions, if I could express, embody their interior convictions, that were indeed life." Men in the abstract are seldom enough. Emerson's notes to himself emphasize particular people. "You must never lose sight of the purpose of helping a particular person in every word you say."

And just as one must have particular people in mind, so one must avoid making empty claims. A good audience will force you to arrange your material so that your arguments are self-evident and validate themselves. "You shall not tell me that your house is of importance in the commercial world. You shall not tell me that you have learned to know men. You shall make me feel that. Else your saying so unsays it."

It is perhaps impossible to do good work without a good audience. It was so for Emerson and so for others he saw around him. "It seems to me that we get our education ended a little too quick in this country," he wrote in his journal.

> As soon as we have learned to read and write and cipher, we are dismissed from school and we set up for ourselves. We are writers and leaders of opinion and we write away without check of any kind, play whatsoever mad prank, indulge whatever spleen or oddity or obstinacy comes into our dear head and even feed our complacency thereon and thus fine wits come to nothing as good horses spoil themselves by running away and straining themselves. I cannot help seeing that Dr. [William Ellery] Channing would have been a much greater writer had he found a strict tribunal of writers, a graduated [i.e., graded] intellectual empire established in the land and knew that bad logic would not pass and that the most severe exaction was to be made on all who enter the lists.

Writers in English do not have the problem of too small a potential audience. Emerson noted in his journal that "Oehlenschlager [A. G., 1779–1850, acclaimed national poet of Denmark] said, that when he wrote in Danish, he wrote to no more than two hundred readers."

Emerson wanted a large audience, an educated and discriminating audience, but he never lost sight of the solitary reader, the single hearer, and this awareness gives his best writing that tone of intimacy which accompanied the clarity and which makes each of his readers feel personally addressed. "Happy is he who looks only into his work to know if it will succeed, never into the times or the public opinion; and who writes from the love of imparting certain thoughts and not from the necessity of sale—who writes always to *the unknown friend*."

Art Is the Path

Though we often think of Emerson as an essayist, his strongest and most lasting self-identification was as a poet. He told Lydia Jackson when he was courting her that poetry was his vocation, noting wryly that his singing was very husky and "is for the most part in prose." By "poet" he meant "verse-maker," and something more. He often used the word to take in what we now mean by "writer," and his essay "The Poet" is arguably the best single piece ever written about expressionism in literature, the idea that expression, including self-expression, is a basic human need, and is the fundamental function of literature.

When he advises young Woodbury to "let the noun do the work," or tells young Henry Thoreau to keep a journal, or tells Elizabeth Peabody precisely how to keep a journal, we see Emerson at his practical best. This is the less well-known, the workshop side of the man. "The Poet" gives us the other, more theoretical, better-known side.

He is only one paragraph into the essay when he proposes a sweeping theory of literature—of art, really. "The poet is representative. He stands among partial men for the complete man, and apprises us not of his wealth, but of the common wealth. The young man reveres men of genius, because, to speak truly, they are more himself than he is."

This is a vehemently anti-elitist view of the artist. The artist, the poet, is not a special or a different kind of person; rather, he or she has developed more completely than most people the poetic impulse all people share. And because we all share this impulse, the poet is assured that communication is at least possible. The poet may be "isolated among his contemporaries by truth and by his art, but with this consolation in his pursuits, that they will draw all men sooner or later. For all men live by truth and stand in need of expression. In love, in art, in avarice, in politics, in labor, in games, we study to utter our painful secret. The man is only half himself, the other half is his expression."

Perhaps "expressing" would be a better choice of words, for Emerson points out that the essential thing about poetry is the process not the product. Thus he insists that the poet is "the sayer, the namer," and pointedly not the maker. Of course he is interested in the end product, the completed poem, but he is comparatively more concerned with how it is all brought about, with the process of poetry. This is because, as he now says, "poetry was all written before time was, and whenever we are so finely organized that we can penetrate into that region where the air is music, we hear those primal warblings and attempt to write them down." The poems were all there before the poet appeared. So Emerson can say "America is a poem in our eyes," and he can argue that the world is a poem, and everything in nature is a poem, if only we can see it, catch it, and write it down. "Nature's first green is gold," writes Robert Frost,

Her hardest hue to hold.
Her early leaf's a flower,
But only so an hour.

The poem is there, in nature, right in front of the poet's eyes. His or her job is first of all to notice and second, to get it down. "For it is not metres," Emerson goes on, "but a metre-making argument that makes a poem,—a thought so passionate and alive that like the spirit of a plant or an animal it has a new architecture of its own and adorns nature with a new thing."

Watching a snowstorm one day, Emerson made notes in his journal:

Announced by all the trumpets of the winds Arrived the snow and driving o'er the field, seems nowhere to alight. The whited air hides hills and woods, the river and the heaven and veils the farmhouse at the garden's end. The traveler stopped and sled the courier's feet delayed all friends shut out the housemates sit Around the radiant fireplace enclosed in a tumultuous privacy of storm. Come see the Northwind's masonry out of an unseen quarry evermore furnished with projected roof round every windward stake and tree and door speeding the myriadhanded his wild work so fanciful so savage nought cares he for number or proportion mockingly on coop and kennel he hangs Parian wreaths A swanlike form invests the hidden thorn Fills up the farmer's lane from wall to wall Maugre the farmer's sighs and at the gates a tapering turret overtops the work Then when his hours are numbered and the world is all his own Retiring as he were not Leaves when the sun appears astonished art to ape in his slow structures stone by stone Built in an age the mad wind's night work The frolic architecture of the snow.

Later he rearranged the prose into a poem:

Announced by all the trumpets of the sky,
Arrives the snow, and, driving o'er the fields,
Seems nowhere to alight: the whited air
Hides hills and woods, the river, and the heaven,
And veils the farm-house at the garden's end.
The sled and traveler stopped, the courier's feet
Delayed, all friends shut out, the housemates sit
Around the radiant fireplace, enclosed
In a tumultuous privacy of storm.

Come see the north wind's masonry.
Out of an unseen quarry evermore
Furnished with tile, the fierce artificer
Curves his white bastions with projected roof
Round every windward stake, or tree, or door.
Speeding, the myriad-handed, his wild work
So fanciful, so savage, nought cares he
For number or proportion. Mockingly,
On coop or kennel he hangs Parian wreaths;
A swan-like form invests the hidden thorn;
Fills up the farmer's lane from wall to wall,
Maugre the farmer's sighs; and at the gate
A tapering turret overtops the work.
And when his hours are numbered, and the world
Is all his own, retiring, as he were not,
Leaves, when the sun appears, astonished Art

To mimic in slow structures, stone by stone,
Built in an age, the mad wind's night work,
The frolic architecture of the snow.

Just when the formalist throws up his hands—are we talking about prose, prose chopped into lines, or poetry here?—Emerson glides like the snowstorm itself over definitions and fences, giving us a concrete performance, a sample of Coleridge's organic form. Emerson's interest is in the workshop phase, the birthing stage of art, not the museum moment, the embalming phase. Poetry mimics Creation and is therefore sacred. More precisely, just as God may indeed be a verb (as Mary Daly insists), poetry is the activity of *creating*. The process of poetry also mimics the process of nature. "This expression or naming is not art, but a second nature, grown out of the first, as a leaf out of a tree. What we call nature is a certain self-regulated motion or change." Another aspect of nature is genius, which, as Emerson observes, "is the activity which repairs the decays of things." His example—and it is a surprising pre-Darwinian, anti-Malthusian one—is from nature, which, as he says, "through all her kingdoms insures herself." Emerson gets specific, is full of enthusiasm, sounds like Carl Sagan. "Nobody cares for planting the poor fungus; so she shakes down from the gills of one agaric [a gill-bearing mushroom or toadstool] countless spores, any one of which, being preserved, transmits new billions of spores tomorrow or next day. The new agaric of this hour has a chance which the old one had not. This atom of seed is thrown into a new place, not subject to the accidents which destroyed its parent two rods off."

As with the agaric, so with humans. Nature "makes a man; and having brought him to a ripe age, she will no longer run the risk of losing this wonder at a blow, but she detaches from him a new self, that the kind may be safe from accidents to which the individual is exposed." As with the agaric and human generations, so Nature handles the poet. "So when the soul of the poet has come to ripeness of thought, she [Nature] detaches and sends away from it poems or songs,—a fearless, sleepless, deathless progeny, which is not exposed to the accidents of the weary kingdom of time."

But we live after all in that "weary kingdom of time," and Emerson's idea of art, of poetry, fits satisfyingly into this world as he says, in the essay's high point and culminating line, "Art is the path of the creator to his work." One cannot repeat it enough; art is not the finished work, art is the getting there. This is why good schools believe in art education, in *doing* art as well as art history. This is why we give children finger paints; it is the process of expressing that we value, along with—or even more than—the finished work, which, as Emerson observes, passes at once into a mortuary state once completed and detached from its creator, unless, like a seed, it be good for starting the process all over again. "The painter, the sculptor, the composer, the epic rhapsodist, the orator, all partake one desire, namely, to express themselves symmetrically and abundantly, not dwarfishly and fragmentarily."

Lest anyone think this is an easy path, Emerson concludes his essay on the poet as he will conclude each chapter in *Representative Men*, with a reminder of the difficulties involved, the heights not reached. Of course he knows how to exhort. "Doubt not, O poet, but persist. Say 'it is in me and shall out.'" But he also knows the real situation. "Stand there, balked and dumb, stuttering and stammering, hissed and hooted, stand and strive, until at last rage draw out of thee that *dream*-power which every night shows thee is thine own."

The Writer

It is difficult to overstate the importance of Emerson's under-standing of the poet as representative, as standing for the poet in each of us. And while we continue to think of his 1836 book *Nature* as his central, necessary book, there is an argu-ment that his 1850 book *Representative Men* is his most useful. Emily Dickinson recognized and welcomed it as "a little gran-ite book you can lean on." Emerson's idea that the great figures in history are each representative of some interest or quality all people share is antimonarchical, antiaristocratic, and anti-Carlylean. Carlyle had argued in *On Heroes, Hero-Worship, and the Heroic in History* (1841) that great people are simply born better and stronger than the rest of us and we should be grateful to be ruled by them. Emerson's quite different idea provides a rationale for both democracy and universal educa-tion. "There is one mind common to all individual men. Every man is an inlet to the same and to all of the same. He that is admitted to the right of reason is made a freeman of the whole estate. What Plato has thought, he may think, what a saint has felt, he may feel; what at any time has befallen any man, he can understand." This representativeness of great people can fairly be called Emerson's central social and religious teaching. The greatness of Jesus is that "alone in all history he estimated the greatness of man. . . . He saw that God incarnates himself in man, and evermore goes forth anew to take possession of his World." As with politics, philosophy, education, and religion, so with literature, with writing.

The final, climactic piece in *Representative Men* is "Goethe, or the Writer," which begins with Emerson saying, "I find a provision, in the constitution of the world, for the writer." The reason for this is his equally bold insistence that "Nature will be reported." Nature, in other words, is self-registering. "All things are engaged in writing their history. The planet, the pebble, goes attended by his shadow. The rolling rock leaves its scratches on the mountain." As Emerson sees it, the writer is the agent of this self-registration of nature. "Men are born to write. The gardener saves every slip, and seed, and peach-stone; his vocation is to be a planter of plants. Not less does the writer attend his affair. Whatever he beholds or experiences, comes to him as a model and sits for its picture." The writer "believes that all that can be thought can be written, first or last; and he would report the Holy Ghost, or attempt it."

It is strangely moving to note that the final entry in Henry Thoreau's grand journal, the entry for November 3, 1861 (he would die on May 6, 1862), is also on this idea of nature's self-registration. "After a violent easterly storm in the night, which clears up at noon, I notice that the surface of the rail-road causeway, composed of gravel, is singularly marked, as if stratified like some slate rocks, on their edges, so that I can tell within a small fraction of a degree from what quarter the rain came. . . . Thus each wind is self-registering."

Nature may indeed be self-registering, just as all the poems may have existed before time began, but it takes an Emerson or a Thoreau to notice and to get it down. "Society has, at all times, the same want, namely of one sane man with adequate powers of expression to hold up each object of monomania in its right relations."

For a Platonist, Emerson has surprisingly little faith in general ideas. An idea must be particular or it is just words. In politics, in art, in argument, or in neighborliness, everything is ad hominem, is only legitimate and real when it comes down to particular people. So, for Emerson, "talent alone cannot make a writer. There must be a man behind the book; a personality which, by birth and quality, is pledged to the doctrine there set forth." For the present essay, the particular person is Goethe, the great German writer who "lived in a small town, in a petty state" and who "appears at a time when a general culture has spread itself and has smoothed down all sharp individual traits." Emerson's choosing Goethe as his final representative figure was the outcome of a long fascination. Margaret Fuller, Emerson's close friend, fellow transcendentalist, and coeditor of *The Dial*, was profoundly interested in Goethe. Emerson learned German in order to read through the complete works of Goethe, which he actually did. He credited Goethe with having "flung into literature, in his Mephistopheles, the first organic figure that has been added for some ages and which will remain as long as the Prometheus." Emerson was also moved by Goethe's emphasis on *Bildung*, self-cultivation or self-development, which is, after all, what Emerson's "Self-Reliance" is all about.

Goethe is also an impressive example of just what it takes to overcome what W. J. Bate called "the burden of the past," the ever-growing awareness of the ever-increasing amount of good work that has already been done, each lick of which makes it all the harder for the current generation to achieve anything at all. As T. S. Eliot put it, "not only every great poet, but every genuine, though lesser, poet, fulfills once for all some possibility of the language, and so leaves one possibility less for his successors." Goethe was acutely aware of this problem. He told his friend Johann Peter Eckermann how glad he was not to be English and in Shakespeare's shadow. "A dramatic talent," Goethe said,

> if it were significant, could not help taking notice of Shakespeare; indeed it could not help studying him. But to study him is to become aware that Shakespeare has already exhausted the whole of human nature in all directions and in all depths and heights, and that for those who come after him, there remains nothing more to do. And where would an earnest soul, capable of appreciating genius, find the courage to set pen to paper, if he were aware of such unfathomable and unreachable excellence already in existence! In that respect I was certainly better off in my dear Germany fifty years ago.

Goethe wouldn't let the subject go. "But had I been born an Englishman, and had those manifold masterworks pressed in upon me with all their power from my first youthful awakening, it would have overwhelmed me, and I would not have known what I wanted to do!"

Goethe was able to talk about this problem only in old age, when he had a secure achievement to his credit. But he could remember how he had felt as a beginner. "It is certain," he told Eckermann, "that if everyone could be made aware early enough how full the world already is of things of highest excellence, and how much is required to set something beside these works that is equal to them, out of a hundred present-day poetic youths scarcely a single one would feel in himself enough perseverance, talent and courage to go on peacefully and achieve a similar masterpiece." Goethe was not speaking about young poets in the abstract. The author of *Faust* was speaking of himself. "Had I known as clearly as I do now how much that is excellent has been in existence for hundreds and thousands of years, I would not have written a line, but would have done something else."

Goethe said this to Eckermann in Germany in February 1826, when the young American Emerson was twenty-three years old, his eyes having failed, forcing him to abandon graduate school. If a great and world-famous artist could feel this way, what must the stumbling young American have felt? The solution would be the same for both. "Goethe teaches courage, and the equivalence of all times; that the disadvantages of any epoch exist only for the fainthearted." Emerson learned, perhaps from Goethe, the same thing. In "Self-Reliance" he puts it this way:

> There is a time in every man's education when he arrives at the conviction that envy is ignorance; that imitation is suicide; that he must take himself for better or worse as his portion; that though the wide universe is full of good, no kernel of nourishing corn can come to him but through his toil bestowed on that plot of ground which is given him to till. The power that resides in him is new in nature, and none but he knows what that is which he can do, nor does he know until he has tried.

That is the mature Emerson, thirty-eight years old in 1841. Here, by way of contrast, is the young twenty-year-old Emerson of 1823 trying desperately to make room for himself at the table and sounding more like Melville's Ahab than like the genteel Emerson so often served up in school: "Who is he that shall control me? Why may not I act and speak and write and think with entire freedom?" Emerson asked his journal. "What am I to the universe, or, the universe, what is it to me?

Who hath forged the chains of wrong and right, of Opinion and Custom? And must I wear them?" The astonishing outpouring and confession roars on:

> I am solitary in the great society of beings. I see the world, human, brute, and inanimate nature—I am in the midst of them, but not of them; I hear the song of the storm. . . . I see cities and nations and witness passions . . . but I partake it not . . . I disclaim them all. . . . I say to the Universe, Mighty one! Thou art not my mother. Return to chaos if thou wilt. I shall exist. I live. If I owe my being, it is to a destiny greater than thine. Star by star, world by world, system by system shall be crushed,—but I shall live."

This is Yankee chutzpah, sheer effrontery and shameless audacity, but it is something more. When Emerson maintained that the divine exists in every person, he was not just restating an article of liberal Christianity; he was putting words to something he felt personally. This outburst is decades before Whitman or Michelet or Melville. This is the cry of an American Prometheus in New England.

Emerson would soon settle for a less Byronic, less Melvillean rhetorical style; he would choose instead the personal immediacy and implied companionship of the Montaigne-like or Bacon-like essay. But the raw and passionate ambition expressed just above was always there, and it could rise to the surface now and then in bold and startling terms, as when Emerson chose to end *Representative Men* with Goethe and with what Goethe taught, that "the world is young, the former great men call to us affectionately. We too must write Bibles, to unite again the heavenly and the earthly world." It had been true for Goethe. Emerson saw it was now true for him. Perhaps it is still true.

Epilogue

No one can maintain the heroic, the Promethean tone all the time. Emerson came to adopt, for most of his writing, a calmer rhetoric, a muted bravado, but a bravado nonetheless, which breaks out from time to time with unexpected heat. Toward the end of *Nature*, for example, Emerson turns directly to his reader and says unblushingly:

> Every spirit builds itself a house, and beyond its house a world, and beyond its world a heaven. Know then, that the world exists for you. For you is the phenomenon perfect. What we are, that only can we see. All that Adam had, all that Caesar could, you have and can do. Adam called his house, heaven and earth; Caesar called his house, Rome; you perhaps call yours, a cobbler's trade; a hundred acres of ploughed land; or a scholar's garret. Yet line for line and point for point, your dominion is as great as theirs, though without fine names. Build, therefore, your own world.

To listen to Emerson was to catch fire. His essays, says Woodbury, are "lyric and a solvent force." Listening to Emerson was for Woodbury like experiencing "dark fires of volcanic regions." But the volcanic, the heroic energy of such a passage as the end of *Nature* just cited was more often muted or hidden, just as the real Emerson was often concealed by the socially observable Emerson. The real Emerson also knew that it required courage for anyone—but especially for a young person—to stand up and say publicly, "I will be a writer." He was well aware, perhaps increasingly aware as he grew older, that such a commitment had a steep cost. A public triumph was a possibility of course, but the more usual and far more predictable outcome was a very different matter. "Thou shalt leave the world, and know the muse only," Emerson writes at the very end of "The Poet." The writer, he says, must "abdicate a manifold and duplex life. . . . Others shall be thy gentlemen and shall represent all courtesy and worldly life for thee. Others shall do the great and resounding actions also. Thou shalt lie close hid with nature and canst not be afforded to the Capitol or the Exchange. The world is full of renunciations and apprenticeships, and this is thine. Thou must pass for a fool and a churl for a long season."

Emerson could accept renunciation because he accepted power, and so had something to renounce. As he puts it in "Self-Reliance," "Life only avails, not the having lived. Power ceases in the instant of repose; it resides in the moment of transition from the past to a new state, in the shooting of the gulf." By power Emerson means not political but personal power, personal energy. Emerson's lifelong quest was for personal power, and Emerson's strength is that he came to understand where his came from. His answer to the question he posed to himself—whence is your power?—is neither pure bravado nor pure renunciation, though it has a little of each. What marks his answer most is its acceptance. The source of his power, he says, is "from my nonconformity. I never listened to your people's laws, or to what they call their gospel, and wasted my time. I was content with the simple rural poverty of my own. Hence this sweetness."

The condition, the challenge, the question, the answer, and the sweetness do not and will not change. It is we who change.

Acknowledgments

Thanks first of all to Joe Parsons, whose interest in this project got me to resurrect and finish it. Amanda Gladin-Kramer transcribed illegible notes, ran down innumerable references, and was an enthusiastic and indispensable research assistant. I will always be grateful for the work—and even more for the friendship and support—of the modern extended transcendental club, including Ron Bosco, Larry Buell, Phyllis Cole, Megan Marshall, Joel Myerson, David Robinson, Nancy Simmons, and Laura Walls. Philip Gura, a leading spirit of that group and a friend for more than thirty years, read the whole manuscript; his encouragement was vital. I'm grateful to Richard Geldard and his Neoplatonic emphasis, to Tim Seldes, who believed in the book from the start, and to Jessie Dolch, who made this a better book. Bruce Boehm made an important discovery; without his help the book would have been sadly delayed. An early version of the chapter "Reading" was published by Sandy McClatchy in *The Yale Review*, vol. 83, no. 1 (January 1995) and titled "Read Only to Start Your Own Team: Emerson on Creative Reading." My wife, Annie Dillard, is my light. "Learn from the masters," she said. I've tried.

Notes

Where possible, I have referred the reader to the two Emerson volumes in the Library of America, *Ralph Waldo Emerson: Essays and Lectures*, ed. Joel Porte (New York: Library of America, 1983), hereafter referred to as Lib of Am 1983; and *Ralph Waldo Emerson: Collected Poems and Translations*, ed. Harold Bloom and Paul Kane (New York: Library of America, 1994), hereafter cited as Lib of Am 1994. Emerson's journal entries are almost entirely from the grand *Journals and Miscellaneous Notebooks of Ralph Waldo Emerson*, ed. William H. Gilman et al., 16 vols. (Cambridge: Harvard University Press, 1960–1982), hereafter JMN.

Introduction
"Meek young men . . . wrote those books": "The American Scholar," Lib of Am 1983, p. 57.
"were never troubled . . . we enter it": JMN 2:219.
"those books . . . their times": JMN 2:265.
"I should like . . . valuable work": Ibid.
"We too . . . Bibles": "Goethe," in *Representative Men*, Lib of Am 1983, p. 761.
"in the long run . . . aim at": Henry D. Thoreau, *Walden* (Princeton: Princeton University Press, 1971), p. 27.
"All things . . . wrong one": "The American Scholar," Lib of Am 1983, p. 54.
"must do . . . cloud of arrows": JMN 10:41.

"Daughters of Time . . . saw the scorn": "Days," in "May-Day and Other Pieces," Lib of Am 1994, p. 178.

"The first rule . . . meant to say": JMN 4:276.

"Good writing . . . perpetual allegories": JMN 5:63.

"All writing . . . dead word": JMN 16:167.

"The thing . . . array of arguments": JMN 5:42.

"Contagion . . . or 'gin'": JMN 9:46.

"All that can . . . be written": JMN 8:438.

"When I look . . . very contemptible": JMN 7:415.

Reading

"There is . . . creative writing": "The American Scholar," Lib of Am 1983, p. 59.

"First we . . . we write": JMN 8:320.

"the student . . . the commentary": "History," Lib of Am 1983, p. 239.

"you are the book's book": "Subjectiveness," part of Emerson's "Philosophy of the People" series of 1866. Manuscript in Houghton Library, Harvard University, bMSAm 1280.209 (12).

"if I had read . . . as ignorant": JMN 2:230.

"If I am . . . by poring": *Essays of Montaigne*, vol. 2, tr. Charles Cotton (London, 1926 [1685]), pp. 86–87.

the hourglass . . . the Golconda: See S. T. Coleridge, 1811–1812, *Lectures on Shakespeare and Milton*, Lecture 2.

"I expect . . . the assimilating power": JMN 8:254.

"It seemed to me . . . me as that": Edward W. Emerson, *Emerson in Concord* (Boston: Houghton Mifflin, 1889), p. 29.

"I push the little . . . in Paradise again": *The Letters of Ralph Waldo Emerson*, vol. 7, ed. Eleanor Tilton (New York: Columbia University Press, 1990), p. 393.

"It is taking . . . displaces me": JMN 8:254.

"I surprised you . . . lie low": JMN 8:71.

"drugged . . . of wisdom": Bliss Perry, *The Heart of Emerson's Journals* (Boston: Houghton Mifflin, 1926), p. 250.

"If a man . . . soon be knowing": JMN 4:372.

"A vast number . . . by the dead": "Literature. First Lecture," in The Present Age series, *Early Lectures of Ralph Waldo Emerson*, vol. 3, ed. S. E. Whicher, Robert E. Spiller, and Wallace E. Williams (Cambridge: Harvard University Press, 1972), p. 210.

"We are too civil . . . hundred pages": JMN 7:457.

"The public necessarily . . . above its model": JMN 5:500. A later version appears in "The Divinity School Address."

"It is always . . . read old books": "Books," in Ralph Waldo Emerson, *Society and Solitude*, centenary ed. (Cambridge: Riverside Press, 1904).

"If Homer . . . avail him nothing": *Early Lectures*, vol. 2 (1964), p. 260.

"A man must . . . to his state": JMN 4:51.

"nothing . . . of his own state": James Joyce, *A Portrait of the Artist as a Young Man* (New York: Modern Library, 1928 [1916]), p. 180.

"What can we see . . . to be born": "Ethics," in *Early Lectures*, vol. 2, p. 149.

"Insist that . . . perhaps Kant will": JMN 5:390. *Early Lectures*, vol. 2, has a reworked version, pp. 260–261.

"It makes no difference . . . American History": JMN 10:34–35.

"Every word . . . every word": JMN 8:157.

"Everything a man knows . . . of himself ": JMN 3:196.

"Philosophers must not . . . not the receiver's": JMN: 5:462.

"What is genius . . . a thousand different things": JMN 6:113.

"Reading is closely . . . limestone condition": Charles J. Woodbury, *Talks with Ralph Waldo Emerson* (New York: Baker and Taylor, 1890), pp. 24–25.

"who are not lazy . . . books of travel too": Ibid., pp. 25–26.

"And there is Darwin . . . see him here": Ibid., p. 26.

"Avoid all . . . your own quarrying": Ibid., p. 27.

"Did you ever . . . what to put in": Ibid., p. 35.

"But have little . . . meant for you": Ibid., pp. 28–29.

"Reading long . . . the first paragraph": Ibid., p. 29.

"Do not attempt . . . the gaze obscures": Ibid., p. 27.

"Well, learn how . . . your own team": Ibid., p. 28.

"unit and universe are round": "Uriel," Lib of Am 1994, p. 16.

"Every spirit . . . your own world": *Nature*, Lib of Am 1983, p. 48.

Keeping a Journal

"Keep a Journal . . . mere conversation": "The Head," in "Human Culture" lecture series, *Early Lectures*, vol. 2, p. 261.

"When I was . . . needed alteration": JMN 7:302.

"He advised me . . . my thoughts, *ready*": Letter from Elizabeth Palmer Peabody to George Peabody, June 18, 1836. I am grateful to Megan Marshall for calling this to my attention.

"My Journals . . . woods and pastures": *The Correspondence of Emerson and Carlyle*, ed. Joseph Slater (New York: Columbia University Press, 1964), p. 272.

Practical Hints

"hitch your wagon to a star": The phrase and the story are in "Civilization," in Emerson, *Society and Solitude*, p. 30.

"I am a rocket-manufacturer": JMN 7:245.

"The way to write . . . arrows are spent": JMN 8:400.

"The only path . . . shall be released": "Worship," in "The Conduct of Life," Lib of Am 1983, p. 1075.

"the great class . . . fools of ideas": Ibid., p. 1074.

"There is no way . . . by writing": Woodbury, *Talks*, p. 139.

"I have read . . . waste of pages": JMN 8:199.

"You should start . . . made it yours": Woodbury, *Talks*, p. 22.

"it is one . . . whole success depends": JMN 4:14.

"In writing . . . expression has escaped": JMN 8:113–114.

"Three or four . . . satellite, and flourish": JMN 9:250.

Nature

"They say much . . . while they lived": JMN 5:290.

"Our age . . . history of theirs": *Nature*, Lib of Am 1983, p. 7.

"the contagion of folly . . . the universe": Quoted in Robert Coles, *Simone Weil* (Reading: Addison Wesley, 1987), p. 100.

"Nature is the vehicle . . . three fold degree": *Nature*, Lib of Am 1983, p. 20.

"Words are signs . . . *raising of the eyebrow*": Ibid.

"The poets made . . . Language is fossil poetry": "The Poet," in *Essays*, 2nd series, Lib of Am 1983, p. 457. See Richard Trench, *On the Study of Words*, 4th ed. (London: Parker and Son, 1853 [1851]).

"Genius . . . decays of things": "The Poet," Lib of Am 1983, p. 457.

"hundreds of writers . . . to visible things": *Nature*, Lib of Am 1983, pp. 22–23.

"Particular natural facts . . . spiritual facts": Ibid., p. 20.

"The world is . . . of the invisible": Ibid., p 24.

"mind is the active . . . the passive": See Daniel Howe, "The Cambridge Platonists of Old England and the Cambridge Platonists of New England," in *American Unitarianism 1805–1865*, ed. Conrad E. Wright (Boston: Massachusetts Historical Society and Northeastern University Press, 1989).

"if our passions . . . the allegory": C. S. Lewis, *The Allegory of Love* (London: Oxford University Press, 1936), p. 45.

"shall see that nature . . . one maxim": "The American Scholar," Lib of Am 1983, p. 56.

"The Universe is . . . of the soul": "The Poet," Lib of Am 1983, p. 453.

"most strangely impressed . . . had accumulated": Theodore
Dreiser, *An American Tragedy* (New York: Limited Editions
Club, 1954 [1926]), ch. XLIV, p. 314.

"What intellect restores . . . set it free": Marcel Proust, *Contre Sainte
Beuve*, in *Marcel Proust on Art and Literature, 1896–1919*, tr. Sylvia
Townsend Warner (Greenwich: Meridian Books, 1958), p. 19.

More Practical Hints

"Over his name . . . under it": "Montaigne," in *Representative Men*,
Lib of Am 1983, p. 699.

"The sincerity . . . vascular and alive": Ibid., p. 700.

"All rising . . . winding stair": Francis Bacon, "Of Great Place," in
Essays (London: Oxford University Press, 1937 [1587]), pp. 45–46.

"Men of age . . . repent too soon": Francis Bacon, "Of Youth and
Age," in *Essays*, p. 175.

"Young men . . . settled business": Ibid., p. 174.

"Things seem . . . somehow answered": "Montaigne," Lib of Am
1983, p. 709.

"The positive degree . . . stupendo": JMN 5:262.

"Avoid adjectives . . . do the work": Woodbury, *Talks*, p. 23.

"It is the best . . . nothing private in it": JMN 7:185.

"Language should aim . . . merely suggest it": JMN 8:180.

"Art lies not . . . are prominent": JMN 11:436.

"Nothing can be added . . . What word can you add": JMN 5:355, 364.

"grinds and grinds . . . flock to our aid": JMN 5:481.

"If you desire . . . three times removed": JMN 7:90.

"An institution . . . one man": "Self-Reliance," Lib of Am 1983, p. 267.

"The most interesting . . . you see it": Woodbury, *Talks*, p. 22.

"'Do not put hinges . . . unnatural to him": Ibid., pp. 154–155.

"Consistency . . . little minds": "Self-Reliance," Lib of Am 1983, p.
265.

"Neither concern yourself . . . scissors meet": Ibid., pp. 23–24.

"All writing is . . . man-making words": JMN 8:148.

"The power . . . orator and poet": In "Art," *Essays*, 1st series, Lib of
Am 1983, p. 433.

"denying, preparing . . . very little": JMN 8:318.

"He is a poor writer . . . courage of treatment": JMN 7:377.

"I dreamed . . . I ate the world": JMN 7:525.

"Power ceases . . . the soul becomes": "Self-Reliance," Lib of Am
1983, p. 271.

"**For the best part . . . his possibility**": JMN 9:341.

"**I lose days . . . should be spent**": JMN 3:103.

"**I soon found . . . finally perform it**": Johnson quoted in JMN 5:248.

"**Always that work . . . not now required**": JMN 7:49.

"**In my memoirs . . . amiability prompted**": JMN 11:434.

"**Our moods . . . continuous pages**": JMN 7 293. The passage also appears in the essay "Circles," *Essays*, 1st series, Lib of Am 1983, p. 406.

"**Since I came . . . a diseased mind**": *Letters of Ralph Waldo Emerson*, vol. 2, ed. Ralph Rusk (New York: Columbia University Press, 1939), pp. 224–225.

"**When I write . . . see it again**": JMN 7:405.

"**A man can . . . read his paper**": JMN 13:348.

"**the vital authority . . . Jews possess**": Lib of Am 1983, p. 652.

"**left France . . . begun again**": Lib of Am 1983, p. 745.

"**It is easy . . . can be justified**": JMN 9:203.

"**I call you . . . exhibitions of wit**": Ibid.

"**Loose the knot . . . help for it**": JMN 10:68–69.

"**My heart's inquiry . . . your power**": JMN 7:342.

"**The one thing . . . high mental energy**": JMN 11:457.

"**I value men . . . go alone**": JMN 11:12.

The Language of the Street

"**Life is our dictionary . . . work-yard made**": "The American Scholar," Lib of Am 1983, pp. 61–62.

"**I ask not . . . of the body**": Ibid., pp. 68–69.

"**should not be addressed . . . *if used***": JMN 4:356.

"**has seen as no other . . . splendid conversation**": JMN 5: 291.

"**Strict conversation . . . writing is drawn**": JMN 8:335.

"**I will tell . . . business-like terms**": *Correspondence of Emerson and Carlyle*, p. 167.

"**Now and then . . . in the street**": JMN 13:312.

"**The plain style . . . share in it**": JMN 13:354.

"**Tell children . . . railroad novels**": JMN 9:405.

Words

One modern critic: The critic is F. O. Matthiessen. See his still challenging assessment of Emerson and language in *American Renaissance* (London: Oxford University Press, 1941), esp. book 1, section I, chapters 4 ("The Word One with the Thing") and 6 ("A Few Herbs and Apples").

"All language . . . for homestead": "The Poet," *Essays*, 2nd series, Lib of Am 1983, p. 463.

"Skill in writing . . . cover a thing": JMN 5:401.

"Scholars . . . to the word": *Early Lectures*, vol. 2, p. 231.

"Chaucer, Milton . . . the inestimable poem": JMN 11:372.

"There is every degree . . . as he is": JMN 5:51.

"I cannot hear . . . mere abstractions": JMN 5:197.

"The true conciseness . . . could illustrate": JMN 7:237.

"What I am in words . . . same in life": Fox quoted in JMN 4:33.

"If I were called . . . word you say": JMN 4:380.

"The art of writing . . . efficient than either": JMN 7:24.

"No man can . . . that is wrong": JMN 3:270–271.

"In good prose . . . one with things": JMN 3: 271.

"never read any . . . a year old": "Books," in *Society and Solitude*, p. 196.

"If a man has . . . in the woods": *Journals of Ralph Waldo Emerson*, ed. E. W. Emerson and W. E. Forbes, 10 vols. (Boston: Houghton Mifflin, 1909–1914), vol. 8, pp. 528–529.

"If I made laws . . . remain silent": JMN 9:17.

"'after all . . . quite a number'": JMN 13:19.

"Literature is . . . intuition or two": "Literature. Second Lecture," in *Early Lectures*, vol. 3, p. 231. As he worked, Emerson was attentive to the smallest changes. JMN 7:120 has "verbs and nouns."

Sentences

"The maker . . . old Night": JMN 4:363.

"Whosoever . . . imply all truth": JMN 4:367.

"My debt to Plato . . . destroy the rest": JMN 5:140.

"He only is . . . contribution of observation": JMN 5:147.

"[Carlyle] believes . . . but half read": JMN 5:291.

"Two proverbs . . . golden saying": JMN 5:342.

"Here I sit . . . repellent particle": *Correspondence of Emerson and Carlyle*, p. 185.

"My thoughts are . . . into Lethe water": JMN 7:327.

"I know not why . . . the whole discourse": JMN 8:36–37.

"[Rabelais'] style . . . exhaustless affluence": JMN 8:290.

"Every man . . . wanted much": "Nominalist and Realist," in *Essays*, 2nd series, Lib of Am 1983, p. 583.

"Meek young men . . . wrote those books": "The American Scholar," Lib of Am 1983, p. 57.

"Every hero . . . at last": "Uses of Great Men," in *Representative Men*, Lib of Am 1983, p. 627.

"Nothing astonishes . . . plain dealing": "Art," in *Essays*, 1st series, Lib of Am 1983, p. 436.

"I wish to write . . . wildest freedom": JMN 7:219.

"All mankind love a lover": "Love," in *Essays*, 1st series, Lib of Am 1983, p. 328.

"Hitch your wagon to a star": "Civilization," in *Society and Solitude*, p. 30.

"Here once . . . round the world": "Hymn Apr 19 1836," Lib of Am 1994, p. 125.

"Things . . . ride mankind": "Ode Inscribed to W. H. Channing," Lib of Am 1994, p. 63.

"If you write . . . path to your door": The eleventh edition of *Bartlett's Quotations* (1938) has a succinct account on p. 416 of how this saying came to be attributed to Emerson.

"A foolish . . . little minds": "Self-Reliance," in *Essays*, 1st series, Lib of Am 1983, p. 265.

"An institution . . . one man": Ibid. p. 267.

"Our chief want . . . what we can": "Considerations by the Way," in *Conduct of Life*, Lib of Am 1983, p. 1093.

Emblem, Symbol, Metaphor

"The schools of poets . . . poets and mystics": "The Poet," in *Essays*, 2nd series, Lib of Am 1983, p. 454.

"The use of symbols . . . all poetic forms": Ibid., p. 461.

"ounce, dice, trice . . . denim": Alistair Reid, *Ounce Dice Trice* (Boston: Little, Brown, 1958).

sacramental or symbolic view": *Sacramentalism* is defined in the *Oxford English Dictionary* as "the theory that the natural world is a reflection of an ideal supernatural world."

"Have mountains . . . of the invisible": *Nature*, Lib of Am 1983, p. 24.

"A Fact . . . invisible world": Ibid., p. 25.

"Things more excellent . . . in every part": "The Poet," in *Essays*, 2nd series, Lib of Am 1983, p. 452.

"The Universe . . . around it": Ibid., p. 453.

"Good writing . . . already made": *Nature*, Lib of Am 1983, p. 23.

"The forms . . . novel assert": William Gass, *Habitations of the Word* (New York: Simon & Schuster, 1985), p. 85.

"It . . . is proper creation": *Nature*, Lib of Am 1983, p. 23.

"The world . . . all are emblems": "The Poet," Lib of Am 1983, p. 456.

"**Barbie emerged . . . catch her breath**": Paul Scott, *The Towers of Silence* (part three of *The Raj Quartet*) (Chicago: University of Chicago Press, 1998 [1972]), p. 67.

"**Barbie sat . . . vaguest picture**": Ibid., p. 68.

"**'Each new law . . . of each man'**": Ibid., p. 84.

Audience

"**To Charles Chauncy Emerson . . . not to be forgotten**": *The Letters of Ralph Waldo Emerson*, vol. 1, ed. Ralph L. Rusk (New York: Columbia University Press, 1939), pp. 238–240.

"**If I could . . . indeed life**": JMN 4:346.

"**You must never . . . word you say**": JMN 4:381.

"**You shall not . . . unsays it**": JMN 7:490.

"**It seems to me . . . enter the lists**": JMN 8:121.

"**Oehlenschlager . . . two hundred readers**": JMN 11:367.

"**Happy is he . . . *the unknown friend***": JMN 10:315.

Art Is the Path

"**is for the most part in prose**": *Letters of Ralph Waldo Emerson*, vol. 1, p. 435.

"**The poet . . . than he is**": "The Poet," Lib of Am 1983, p. 448.

"**isolated among his . . . is his expression**": Ibid.

"**poetry was all . . . write them down**": Ibid., p. 449.

"**America is a poem in our eyes**": Ibid., p. 465.

"**Nature's first . . . so an hour**": Robert Frost, *New Hampshire* (New York: Henry Holt, 1923).

"**For it is not . . . a new thing**": "The Poet," Lib of Am 1983, p. 450.

"**Announced . . . architecture of the snow**": The prose version of the poem is in JMN 6:246. The poem is in Lib of Am 1994.

"**This expression . . . motion or change**": "The Poet," Lib of Am 1983, p. 457.

"**is the activity . . . two rods off**": Ibid.

"**makes a man . . . kingdom of time**": Ibid., pp. 447–448.

"**Art is the path . . . to his work**": Ibid., p. 466.

"**The painter . . . and fragmentarily**": Ibid.

"**Doubt not . . . is thine own**": Ibid., pp. 466–467.

The Writer

"**a little . . . can lean on**": *The Letters of Emily Dickinson*, ed. Thomas Johnson and Theodora Ward (Cambridge: Harvard University Press, 1958), p. 569.

"There is one mind . . . he can understand": "History," Lib of Am 1983, p. 237.

"alone in all history . . . of his World": "The Divinity School Address," Lib of Am 1983, p. 80.

"I find a provision . . . the writer": "Goethe," Lib of Am 1983, p. 746.

"Nature will . . . on the mountain": Ibid.

"Men are born . . . or attempt it": Ibid., pp. 746–747.

"Society has . . . right relations": Ibid., p. 748.

"talent alone . . . there set forth": Ibid., p. 756.

"lived in a small . . . individual traits": Ibid., p. 751.

"flung into . . . the Prometheus": Ibid., p. 754.

"not only every . . . for his successors": Quoted by W. J. Bate, *The Burden of the Past and the English Poet* (Cambridge: Harvard University Press, 1970), p. 4.

"A dramatic talent . . . wanted to do": Ibid., p. 6.

"It is certain . . . done something else": Ibid., p. 96.

"Goethe teaches courage . . . the fainthearted": "Goethe," Lib of Am 1983, p. 761.

"There is a time . . . he has tried": "Self-Reliance," Lib of Am 1983, p. 259.

"Who is he . . . I shall live": JMN 2:189–190.

"the world is young . . . earthly world": "Goethe," Lib of Am 1983, p. 761.

Epilogue

"Every spirit builds . . . your own world": *Nature*, Lib of Am 1983, p. 48.

"lyric and a solvent force": Woodbury, *Talks*, p. 155.

"dark fires of volcanic regions": Ibid., p. 143.

"Thou shalt leave . . . a long season": "The Poet," Lib of Am 1983, p. 467.

"Life only avails . . . the gulf ": "Self-Reliance," Lib of Am 1983, p. 271.

"from my nonconformity . . . this sweetness": JMN 8:149.

Index